Standards-Based Leadership

Other Books by the Authors

A School for Every Child: School Choice in America Today

Bullying: The Bullies, the Victims, the Bystanders

Changing Mindsets of Educational Leaders to Improve Schools: Voices of Doctoral Students

Conflicts in Culture: Strategies to Understand and Resolve the Issues

Standards-Based Leadership: A Case Study Book for the Assistant Principalship

Standards-Based Leadership: A Case Study Book for the Principalship

Standards-Based Leadership: A Case Study Book for the Superintendency

The Challenges of No Child Left Behind: Understanding the Issues of Excellence, Accountability, and Choice

Winning Women: Stories of Award-Winning Educators

Standards-Based Leadership

A Case Study Book for the Principalship

Second Edition

Sandra Harris, Julia Ballenger,
and Cynthia Cummings

ROWMAN & LITTLEFIELD
Lanham • Boulder • New York • London

Published by Rowman & Littlefield
A wholly owned subsidiary of The Rowman & Littlefield Publishing Group, Inc.
4501 Forbes Boulevard, Suite 200, Lanham, Maryland 20706
www.rowman.com

Unit A, Whitacre Mews, 26-34 Stannary Street, London SE11 4AB

British Library Cataloguing in Publication Information Available

Library of Congress Cataloging-in-Publication Data

Harris, Sandra, 1946–
Standards-based leadership : a case study book for the principalship / Sandra Harris, Julia Ballenger, and Cynthia Cummings.—Second edition.
pages cm
Includes bibliographical references.
ISBN 978-1-4758-1691-4 (cloth : alk. paper) — ISBN 978-1-4758-1692-1 (pbk. : alk. paper) — ISBN 978-1-4758-1693-8 (electronic)
1. School superintendents—United States—Case studies. 2. Educational leadership—United States—Case studies. 3. Education—Standards—United States—Case studies. 4. School superintendents—United States—Case studies. 5. Educational leadership—United States—Case studies. 6. Education—Standards—United States—Case studies. I. Title.
LB2831.92.H363 2015
371.2'012—dc23
2015006693

Printed in the United States of America

Dr. Sandra Lowery was an author of the first edition of this book. She was a teacher, elementary principal, secondary principal, superintendent, and university professor. Dr. Lowery was a colleague, a dear friend, and a role model for educators. No matter how difficult the challenges in education or in life, she never gave up pursuing her dream to make the world a better place at home, at school, or in her community. Some people **leave** a legacy of greatness, but Sandra Lowery **lived** a legacy of greatness. We dedicate the second edition of this book to Dr. Sandra Lowery and thus to educators everywhere who have that same dream.

Contents

Foreword

The responsibilities of principals and superintendents have changed significantly over the last decade. Policy initiatives like No Child Left Behind and the federal Race to the Top program have refocused the work of educational leadership around student learning. States across the country have set higher expectations for student growth and achievement, placing new demands on district and school leaders to ensure all students are learning. Principals in most states are implementing higher learning standards to prepare all students for college, careers, and life.

Not only have expectations for school leaders increased, but new knowledge also has been gained through research. For example, evidence links education leadership with student performance. It is one of the most important school-based contributors to student achievement. In fact, studies find no documented instances of failing schools turning around without powerful leadership.

Our increased understanding of the role of leadership and the new demands on leaders have significant implications for the practice of school and district leaders as well as the programs that prepare them, implications that exposed the shortcomings of national leadership standards. These new demands are of chief concern to the designers of the 2015 leadership practice (Interstate School Leaders Licensure Consortium [ISSLC]) and preparation (National Educational Leadership Preparation [NELP]) standards. The standards prioritize leadership domains that pertain to a school's instructional program, culture, and human capital management. Together the refreshed ISSLC and NELP standards will further clarify roles and responsibilities for educational leaders, guiding what they are expected to do in their daily work, as well as how they are prepared, and on what they will be evaluated.

However, just as important as the focus of leadership preparation programs is delivery. The learning activities that have traditionally been employed in higher education are lectures, whole-class discussion, and assigned readings. Students will always need ways to acquire information and ideas relevant to the subject of the course, and there will always be value in lectures and readings when studying a given topic. However, students also need opportunities to authentically apply knowledge. The manuscript you are about to explore offers a bridge from the traditional higher education classroom to authentic leadership practice.

Teaching with cases places learning in the center. Cases provide the opportunity for active learning around critical problems of leadership practice. Teaching with cases is an instructional strategy called problem-based learning, and it is used within a variety of higher education programs that prepare adults for professional practice. Ideally, the case reflects a problem that students would encounter in their professional work. Courses that incorporate cases into the core curriculum enable students to analyze specific leadership situations, engage in problem finding and problem framing, identify information and data needs, frame scenarios for action, and assess outcomes. By working in groups, students are able to engage in reflective dialogue and consider the problem from a variety of perspectives.

Regardless of the focus of any given case, they provide the opportunity for aspiring leaders to develop critical leadership skills. The cases included in this text complement this important instructional strategy by targeting critical leadership topics and situations that reflect the context of contemporary leadership. Educational leaders are expected to have a level of readiness on day one, and that readiness is dependent upon the preparation they have received. Preparation programs need high-quality standards-based resources to guide the development and implementation of their programs. This book, which is aligned to both the Texas competencies and the national leadership preparation standards, provides an opportunity for knowledge and skill development. Without question it is an important tool for developing future leaders.

Michelle Young
January 28, 2015

NOTE

Michelle Young is the executive director of the University Council for Educational Administration and a professor of leadership at the University of Virginia. Young serves as the chair of the National Educational Leadership Preparation (NELP) standards committee.

Introduction

Why would I want to exit the classroom to sit in an office marked "Principal"? Why leave behind chalk dust on my pants, riveting class discussions, teenage zits and zest, grading essays, and "ah ha" moments? I would be trading tranquility for turbulence. What was I thinking? The answer is simple. Leading people on a larger scale was my destination.

—Tim Brady (Harris 2006, 8)

There is no doubt that the principal plays a critical role in the fundamental goal of a school: nurture student learning. Today's school principal is charged with the responsibility for creating the kind of learning organization that emphasizes success for all students. This is a huge responsibility that transcends basic managerial duties to embrace complex leadership behaviors that focus on instruction, student diversity, initiation of change, a rapidly growing knowledge base, ever-changing technologies, personnel decisions, and problem solving, to name just a few. Consequently, how the principal prioritizes leadership skills to be an effective administrator is critical to the overall success of the school. The principal must understand how to support teachers, how to promote student learning, and how to engage with the larger community. All of which is done under a critical spotlight often more focused on blaming than building. Indeed, it is the principal who is "central to the task of building schools that promote powerful teaching and learning for all students" (Davis, Johnson-Reid, Saunders, Williams, and Williams 2005, 8).

1

HISTORY OF THE PRINCIPAL ROLE

The position of the principal today is challenging, exacerbated by the tremendous change occurring in our twenty-first-century society. For example, in the early twentieth century, schools were small and ungraded, and teachers performed administrative, clerical, and janitorial tasks that came with running the school (Pierce 1935). The principal (then called the headmaster) kept attendance, reported to the lay school committee, and made sure the building was maintained (Knezevich 1969). By the 1900s the principal had increasing responsibilities in the day-to-day management of the school (Pierce 1935), and according to Tyack and Hansot (1982), the role of the principal "had gravitated from the part-time educational evangelist of the mid-nineteenth century to a new breed of professional managers, who made education a life-long career and who reshaped the schools according to the canons of business efficiency and scientific expertise" (120).

In the 1920s the principal accepted and promoted certain values and worked to connect spiritual issues with those of scientific management (Beck and Murphy 1993). In fact, Cubberley (1923) ascribed the role of the principal as being like that of "the priest in the parish" (26). The 1930s saw the principal as a financial manager, while the 1940s viewed the role as that of a democratic leader (Barnard 1938; Beck and Murphy 1993). In the 1950s the role of applying laws, such as *Brown v. Board of Education of Topeka*, in combination with implementing school activities, increased (Beck and Murphy 1993). The principal of the 1960s found the role more bureaucratic than ever before, while the role of the principal in the 1970s was best described as a humanistic facilitator (Haynen 1973). The 1980s cast the principal into the role of instructional leader, yet since the 1990s the principal role has emphasized that of leader rather than manager.

THE ROLE OF THE PRINCIPAL TODAY

Considering history, there was a time when the principal could be successful if he or she was a good manager. But today's twenty-first-century principal must be all things to all people—an individual who views every action through a magnifying glass while setting the tone for the school climate and culture. The modern principal spends too much time in areas that have little to do with students, such as paperwork, and endless meetings and activities. Studies (Educational Research Service 2000; Harris, Arnold, Lowery, and

Crocker 2000; Moore 2000; Pounder and Merrill 2001) have cited a number of reasons associated with the difficulty of the principalship, all related to the increasingly complex society of today that include the following:

- Increased workload
- Supervision of night activities
- Sixty- to eighty-hour workweek
- Paperwork required by state and district mandates
- Difficulty of satisfying a diverse group of stakeholders
- Insufficient compensation
- Too much stress
- Societal problems that make it difficult to focus on instruction
- Increased litigation
- Discipline issues

Cordeiro and Cunningham (2013) emphasize that the demand today is for a principal who is "a new kind of leader focused on instructional leadership, school improvement, and student achievement with an emphasis on high academic standards and expectations" (9).

In addition, a 2013 report from the Wallace Foundation noted that principal leadership is second only to teacher quality as a priority for school reform. Thus, added to the already complex role of the principal is that of leading state policy regarding licensing and even on-the-job training of principals. Federal efforts such as Race to the Top are also emphasizing that it is the principal's responsibility to boost teaching and learning to transform troubled schools. Overall, the role of the twenty-first-century principal can be synthesized into three primary responsibilities:

- Understanding how to support teachers;
- Managing the curriculum to promote student learning; and
- Transforming schools into more effective organizations that highlight powerful teaching and learning for all students (Davis, Darling-Hammond, LaPointe, and Myerson 2005).

It is no wonder that many principals are considering leaving the position for another career or retiring early.

RECRUITMENT AND RETENTION OF PRINCIPALS

Because of the complexity of the principal's job, attracting and keeping principals is an issue occurring in too many school districts across the country. This "churn and burn" strategy takes its toll on the principalship. Larry Cuban (2010) reported that 61 percent of the lowest-performing schools have had three or more principals since 2000. In fact, 64 percent of high school principals only stay three years before leaving for another assignment.

In many states, half of all beginning principals leave within five years. Added to this, along with natural attrition and retirements, Samuels (2012) indicated about 12 percent of principals who are new to a school leave within the first year and nearly 11 percent leave within the second year. If test scores were low in the new principal's first year, she is even more likely to leave. Richard Flanary, then senior director of professional development for the National Association of Secondary School Principals (NASSP), said, "It takes at least three years for a principal to really get the lay of the land and feel comfortable enough to make progress" (10).

WHY WOULD ANYONE WANT TO BE A PRINCIPAL?

While universities and school districts look for solutions to retain and recruit principals, certainly they must address the barriers that create the stress and difficulty of the job. Yet it is important that the key role the principal plays in the school be reaffirmed, for despite the complexities of the job, current principals love what they do. What attracts men and women to the position of principal? Educators at all levels of schooling agree that the principal is a key player in creating successful, high-performing schools. The job may be difficult, but it offers a valuable opportunity to improve children's lives.

Numerous studies have reported that most individuals entering the principalship are motivated by a desire to make a positive difference in the lives of children (Harris, Arnold, Lowery, and Crocker 2000; Moore 2000; Pounder and Merrill 2001). Thus, a key motivating factor for individuals seeking this job and keeping it is the intrinsic reward of supporting teachers to help young people be successful. Harris (2005, 2006) surveyed sixty-nine award-winning elementary and secondary school principals throughout the United States. The most effective leadership roles these principals acknowledged included the following responsibilities:

- Strengthen leadership to set direction, develop people, and redesign the organization.
- Shape and define a positive campus culture.
- Communicate to collaborate effectively with all stakeholders.
- Encourage and oversee authentic instruction for all students.
- Implement student-centered school improvement strategies.
- Personalize the learning environment for all students. (209–210)

Working between seventy and eighty-plus hours each week, these principals understood what effective schools are about. They knew the importance of working together with others—it's about WE, not ME; they believed that education is about supporting students and not about the school as an institution; and they understood that when they position PEOPLE to become successful they make the world a better place.

Considering the difficult yet critical nature of the job and the problem of recruiting and retaining good principals, it is important that university preparation programs train principals in the reality of the job. It is equally important that practicing principals have resources available to them for continued learning in the field.

THE ROLE OF REFLECTION IN PRINCIPAL PREPARATION

Educator preparation programs have traditionally been structured on the premise that learning to be a teacher or an administrator is a process of acquiring teacher/administrator knowledge, "deposit-making," as opposed to posing the problems of human beings in their relation with the world (Freire 1992, 60). At the same time, individuals new to teaching or administrating are typically most concerned with surviving; thus, reflection is rare (Wideen, Mayer-Smith, and Moon 1998). Consequently, students too often are not able to connect university classroom learning with the real experiences that occur (Harris 2000). However, adult learners enter educational programs with a great diversity of experience (Knowles 1990), and when reflective activities are connected to real-life experiences, "real life meaning" increases (Harris 2000, 24; Kasworm and Marienau 1997).

Relatedly, as individuals construct meanings from their own experiences (Dewey 1938), the idea of reflection-in-action becomes knowing-in-action (Schon 1987). Thus, a valuable activity for principals is to reflect on experiences of the school day. This process contributes to trying out new ideas, affirms or changes decisions, and leads to experience as a resource for continuing education (Clandinin and Connelly 2000). In fact, Clandinin and Connelly (1994) suggested that "to study education . . . is to study experience" (415).

THE ROLE OF STANDARDS IN PRINCIPAL PREPARATION

In 1988 the National Policy Board for Educational Administration (NPBEA) was formed by ten professional educator organizations with the purpose of collectively advancing professional standards for school administration. An additional goal was to develop a common set of guidelines for the National Council for the Accreditation of Teacher Education (NCATE) accreditation of advanced programs in Educational Leadership (NPBEA 2001). The Educational Leadership Constituent Council (ELCC) was then formed to evaluate university programs seeking NCATE accreditation (Wilmore 2002).

In 1994 the Council of Chief State School Officers (CCSSO) developed the Interstate School Leaders Licensure Consortium (ISLLC). This group was charged with developing criteria for states to collaboratively redefine standards of school leadership (Murphy and Shipman 1998; Wilmore 2002). Although ISLLC and NCATE standards were similar, it was awkward working from two separate frameworks. In 2001 the revision of the ELCC guidelines incorporated the ISLLC standards, and these revised standards were adopted by NCATE (NPBEA 2001). Later, with the approval of the ISLLC 2008 standards, the NPBEA approved an ELCC plan to revise the ELCC standards. In 2010 NCATE and the Teacher Education Accreditation Council (TEAC) (another accrediting body) created a single accrediting body for educator preparation called Council for Accreditation of Educator Preparation (CAEP).

The ELCC standards have most recently been updated in 2011 (see appendix 1 and www.ncate.org). The 2014 ISLLC Standards Refresh Project are policy standards that provide direction and guidance to school leaders for today (See Council of Chief State School Officers website at www.ccsso.org).

There is a strong belief that administrators must be held accountable just as teachers. Consequently, there are established educational administrative licensure requirements in all states in the United States. Over forty states require at least a master's degree that includes some administrative courses for an administrative or supervisory license (Cordeiro and Cunningham 2013).

At least thirteen states use an assessment called the School Leadership Licensure Assessment (SLLA) which is based on ISLLC standards and a required component of the administrative licensure process. Many of these states require a state assessment to be completed with a minimal pass score as a prerequisite to receiving a state license (Cordeiro and Cunningham 2013). For example, the Texas State Board of Educator Certification (SBEC) has adopted nine competencies for principals in a state competency licensure exam that are divided into three domains: leadership of the educational community, instructional leadership, and administrative leadership (see appendix 3).

The ELCC standards most recently updated in 2011 (appendix 1), the Texas competencies (appendix 3), and 2014 Texas Principal Standards (appendix 2) and standards from other states are further broken down into smaller behavioral components or elements that are outcome based. Thus, when educators reflect on the events of the day, they self-inspect their actions. When their reflections and subsequent self-inspections are framed within standards rather than being limited to their own experiences, they are able to self-correct by making research-based, best-practice decisions based on the standards (see Figure I.1).

CASE STUDY METHODS

According to Shulman (1996), case methods allow students to focus on real problems and develop a repertoire to guide their thinking and reflections on

Reflection → Critical Self-Inspection → Self-Correction

Framed within Standards

Fig. I.1.

their own actions. Their own experiences become "lenses for thinking about their work" (199) since analyzing the how and why of experiences is critical to effective learning. In fact, the very act of reflecting on experience implies a preparation for the future (Clandinin and Connelly 1991) because it guides metacognitive processes and guides future action (Brubacher, Case, and Reagan 1994).

A key value of reflection is that it offers a "process of solving problems, making decisions, and settling direction" (Brubacher, Case, and Reagan 1994, 91), an especially valuable process for the open-ended problems that educators often face. Only recently has the case study method been used in educational administration preparation programs, although since the mid-1950s, simulations and in-basket activities have been used to enhance the lecture method, which has typically been the primary instructional delivery model in school administration (McCarthy 1999).

The case study method provides opportunities for principals in preparation as well as practicing principals to reflect on the conflicts in administrative decision making. Case studies provide leaders with a framework in which to examine their own values and test these values within the organizational setting. Additionally, cases allow students to "explore approximations of reality" in individual reflection and group dialogue while enabling the learner to "examine a base of data that stands still for examination" (Storey 2001, 7).

When used in a classroom setting, the case study method serves several purposes, such as teaching new information inductively by having students read a case that models the concept and then noting associations between certain factors. Another purpose is as a critical thinking, problem-solving vehicle for applying acquired knowledge to specific situations (Kowalski 2001). Still another purpose encourages synthesizing information as students are asked to combine a variety of factors, including time, ideas, data, community gatekeepers, and many others, in the process of decision making. Clearly, the case study method provides an opportunity for students and practicing principals to build a repertoire of skills in dealing with open-ended problems that characterize the principalship.

STRATEGIES FOR DISCUSSING THE CASE STUDY

According to Kowalski (1999), leaders confronted with problems demanding action may choose one of several behaviors: ignoring the situation, acting instinctively, getting someone else to decide, duplicating something that someone else has done under similar circumstances, or using the professional knowledge base to guide decisions. When using case studies as a learning strategy, participants must have a clear understanding that there may be more than one best answer to the case. Therefore, by encouraging active participation of everyone in the class, discussion should generate several ways to consider the problem and a variety of strategies to solve the problem.

One paradigm that lends itself to case study decision-making strategies includes four steps (Romm and Mahler 1986): define the problem, diagnose the problem, search for alternative solutions, and evaluate alternative solutions. Using these strategies to guide the case study procedure, we recommend that the following nine steps be used for each case study:

1. *Create a climate of trust within the classroom.* Students should be encouraged to be creative, have the freedom to risk an idea, and be able to fail without fear of repercussion in the classroom setting.
2. *Read the case carefully.* Good reading strategies should be followed. First, read to get a clear sense of the issue. Then reread, underlining/ highlighting key ideas and taking notes in the margins or on a separate sheet of paper.
3. *Identify the primary problem.* While the case may describe many problems, it is important to analyze the case to identify the central problem at hand within the framework of the standards.
4. *Identify related problems.* Too often in decision making, we attempt to solve the immediate problem, which is often not the primary issue. For example, if teachers are arguing about a curriculum issue and it is causing disruption on the entire campus, this could be treated as a communication problem. However, on further analysis, one would see that the communication problem is secondary to the primary problem, which is the absence of a shared vision of the school's purpose among the faculty.
5. *Discuss the problem by relating it back to the standard.* What is the standard at issue? If it is primarily a "shared vision" problem, the standards recommend actions regarding how a principal can implement a shared vision on campus. Because the standards are based on best practices and grounded in the literature, these behavioral components should serve as the guiding actions to follow.

6. *Discuss the problem by relating it back to the literature.* It is important in class discussion and analysis that students are guided back to the literature based on research for support. This will legitimize the dialogue and lead to best-practice strategies being implemented rather than acting solely on "opinion" based on limited personal experiences.

7. *Develop strategies.* When developing strategies based on standards, it is important to identify circumstances where and when those strategies will most likely be successful. For example, similar problems in large and small schools might be solved by differing strategies. Do not settle on one possible strategy after it has been identified but, rather, develop alternative strategies.

8. *Evaluate strategies.* Carefully consider strategies that have been identified. What are the strengths of each suggestion, and what are the weaknesses? How could the principal overcome inherent challenges within a situation?

9. *Make a decision.* The role of leadership is decisive. Principals must be able to make a decision, support the decision, and outline specific strategies for implementation that will best result in a positive solution.

HOW TO USE THIS BOOK

The case studies included in this book are based on real problems that have faced real principals. Each chapter uses the following format: (a) identification of Texas competency, 2014 Texas Principal Standards, and 2011 ELCC standards, (b) abstract, (c) objectives, (d) brief literature review, (e) case, (f) discussion questions, (g) additional case to consider on your own, (h) a key statement to remember, (i) references, and (j) additional resources.

We have chosen to use the Texas competencies to focus each chapter. However, if you are practicing in another state, simply relate your state standards or assessment competencies to the 2011 ELCC Standards in this book to discuss the various chapters. Students are encouraged to first discuss each case within the framework of the major competency and standard. As the discussion becomes more in-depth, certainly other competencies and standards will contribute substantially to the case, as it is rarely possible to isolate strategies to just one standard. Because technology is so vital to educational programs today, we also direct you to the International

Society for Technology in Education (ISTE) website. (See www.ISTE.org/standards).

The literature reviews that precede each case provide only an introduction to discussion possibilities. Table I.1 provides a crosswalk for linking the case studies in each chapter to the Texas competencies, 2014 Texas Principal Standards, and the 2011 ELCC Standards. Copies of a complete set of 2011 ELCC standards, 2014 Texas Principal Standards, and Texas test competencies are included in the appendices.

Table I.1. Standards Crosswalk

Chapter	Texas Principal Exam Competencies	TAC – Stds. for Principal Cert. - 2014	ELCC – Standards 2011
1	1 – Shape campus culture by facilitating development, articulation, implementation, and stewardship of shared vision.	4 – School Campus Culture	1 – shared vision; 2 – school culture and instruction
2	2 – Communicate and collaborate with school community, respond to diversity, and mobilize resources.	2 – Human Capital; 3 – Executive Leadership	4 – collaboration and diverse community interests/needs
3	3 – Act with integrity, fairness, and in an ethical and legal manner.	3 - Executive Leadership	4 – collaboration and diverse community interests/needs; 5 – integrity, fairness, and ethical
4	4 – Design and implement curricula and strategic plans that enhance teaching and learning: ensure alignment of curriculum, instruction, resources, and assessment; measure performance.	1 – Instructional Leadership	2 – school culture and instruction
5	5 – Advocate, nurture, and sustain instructional program and campus culture conducive to student learning and staff professional development.	1 – Instructional Leadership; 3 – Executive Leadership; 4 – School Culture	1 – shared vision for a school; 2 – school culture and instruction; 6 – political, social economics, legal and cultural
6	6 – Implement staff evaluation and development system to improve performance of staff, select and implement models for supervision and staff development, and apply legal requirements for personnel management.	1 – Instructional Leadership; 2 – Human Capital	3 – management of organization
7	7 – Apply organizational, decision-making, and problem-solving skills to ensure effective learning.	1 – Instructional Leadership; 5 – Strategic Operations	6 – political, social economics, legal and cultural

Chapter	Texas Principal Exam Competencies	TAC – Stds. for Principal Cert. - 2014	ELCC – Standards 2011
8	8 – Apply principles of leadership and management to campus budgeting, personnel, resource utilization, financial management, and technology.	3 – Executive Leadership	3 – management of organization
9	9 – Apply principles of leadership and management to the campus physical plant and support systems to ensure a safe and effective learning environment.	3 – Executive Leadership	3 – management of organization

REFERENCES

Barnard, C. I. 1938. The functions of the executive. Cambridge, MA: Harvard University Press.

Beck, L. G., and J. Murphy. 1993. Understanding the principalship: Metaphorical themes, 1920s–1990s. New York: Columbia University Teachers College Press.

Brubacher, J. W., C. W. Case, and T. G. Reagan. 1994. Becoming a reflective educator: How to build a culture of inquiry in the schools. Thousand Oaks, CA: Corwin Press.

Clandinin, D. J., and F. M. Connelly. 1991. Narrative and story in practice and research. In The reflective turn: Case studies in and on educational practice (258–81). Edited by D. Schoen. New York: Teachers College Press.

———. 1994. Personal experience methods. In Handbook of qualitative research (413–27). Edited by N. Denzin and Y. Lincoln. Thousand Oaks, CA: Sage.

———. 2000. Narrative inquiry: Experiences and story in qualitative research. San Francisco: Jossey-Bass.

Cordeiro, P. A. and W.G. Cunningham. 2013. Educational leadership: A bridge to improved practice. Boston: Pearson.

Cuban, L. 2010. Principal turnover: "Burn and churn" strategies and student academic achievement. larrycuban.wordpress.com/2010/04/24/principal-turnover-burn-a.

Cubberley, E. P. 1923. Public school administration. Boston: Houghton Mifflin.

Davis, L., M. Johnson-Reid, J. Saunders, J. Williams, and T. Williams. 2005. Academic self-efficacy among African American youths: Implications for school social work practice. Children & Schools 27: 5–14.

Davis, S., L. Darling-Hammond, M. LaPointe, and D. Meyerson. 2005. School leadership study: Developing successful principals (Review of Research). Stanford, CA: Stanford University, Stanford Educational Leadership Institute.

Dewey, J. 1938. Logic: The theory of inquiry. New York: Henry Holt.

Educational Research Service. 1998. Is there a shortage of qualified candidates for openings in the principalship? An exploratory study. Alexandria, VA: National Association of Elementary School Principals; Reston, VA: National Association of Secondary School Principals.

———. 2000. The principal, keystone of a high-achieving school: Attracting and keeping the leaders we need. Arlington, Va.: Educational Research Service.

Freire, P. 1992. Pedagogy of the oppressed. 20th ed. New York: Continuum.

Fullan, M. 1997. What's worth fighting for in the principalship. New York: Harper & Row.

Goodnough, A. 2000. Mrs. Clinton proposes grants for principals. New York Times, September 8, A25.

Harris, S. 2000. The use of experience in reflective scenarios in administrator preparation. Journal of Intermountain Center for Educational Effectiveness 1, no. 2: 20–27.

Harris, S. 2005. Best practices of award-winning elementary principals. Thousand Oaks, CA: Corwin Press.

Harris, S. 2006. Best practices of award-winning secondary principals. Thousand Oaks, CA: Corwin Press.

Harris, S., M. Arnold, S. Lowery, and C. Crocker. 2000. Deciding to become a principal: What factors motivate or inhibit that decision? ERS Spectrum 18, no. 2: 40–45.

Haynen, R. V. 1973. Special leaders needed for special problems. NASSP Bulletin 57, no. 374: 89–92.

Hood, L. 2001. Texas schools are facing huge exodus of principals. San Antonio Express-News, July 22, A1, A19.

Kasworm, C., and C. Marienau 1997. Principles for assessment of adult learning. New Directions for Adult and Continuing Education 75: 5–16.

Knezevich, S. J. 1969. Administration of public educatioin. 2nd ed. New York: Harper & Row.

Knowles, M. 1990. The adult learner: A neglected species. 4th ed. Houston: Gulf.

Kowalski, T. 1999. The school superintendent: Theory, practice and cases. Upper Saddle River, NJ: Prentice Hall.

———. 2001. Case studies on educational administration. 3rd ed. New York: Longman.

McCarthy, M. 1999. The evolution of educational leadership preparation programs. In Handbook of research on educational administration (119–39). 2nd ed. Edited by L. Murphy and K. Louis. San Francisco: Jossey-Bass.

Moore, D. 2000. The vanishing principals: Perceptions of graduate students in two university leadership programs. Journal of the Intermountain Center for Educational Effectiveness 1, no. 1: 11–14.

Murphy, J., and N. Shipman. 1998. The interstate school leaders' licensure consortium: A standards-based approach to strengthening educational leadership. Paper presented at the annual conference of the American Educational Research Association, San Diego, California, April 1998.

National Policy Board for Educational Administration (NPBEA). 2001. Advanced programs in educational leadership for principals, superintendents, curriculum directors, and supervisors. Washington, DC: National Policy Board for Educational Administration.

Pellicer, L. 1999. Caring enough to lead: Schools and the sacred trust. Thousand Oaks, CA: Corwin Press.

Pierce, P. R. 1935. The origin and development of the public school principalship. Chicago: University of Chicago Press.

Pounder, D., and R. Merrill. 2001. Job desirability of the high school principalship: A job choice theory perspective. Educational Administration Quarterly 37, no. 1: 27–57.

Principal Leadership. 2002. Principal shortage, funding concerns drive NASSP board to take a stand. Principal Leadership 50, no. 1: 5.

Romm, T., and S. Mahler. 1986. A three-dimensional model for using case studies in the academic classroom. Higher Education 15, no. 6: 677–96.

Samuels, C. A. 2012. Study: Principal turnover bodes poorly for schools. Education Week 31, no. 23: 10.

Schon, D. 1987. Educating the reflective practitioner. San Francisco: Jossey-Bass.

Sergiovanni, T. 2001. The principalship: A reflective practice perspective. 4th ed. Boston: Allyn & Bacon.

Shulman, L. S. 1996. Just in case: Reflections on learning from experience. In The case for education: Contemporary approaches for using case methods (197–217). Edited by J. Colbert, P. Desbert, and K. Trimble. Needham Heights, MA: Allyn & Bacon.

Steinberg, J. 2000. Nation's schools struggling to find enough principals. New York Times, September 3, A1, A4.

Storey, V. 2001. Dean, judge, and bishop: Lessons from a conflict and implications for school leaders. International Electronic Journal for Leadership in Learning 5, no. 17: 1–14. Available at www.ucalgary.ca/~iejll/volume5/storey.html.

Tyack, D. B., and E. Hansot. 1982. Managers of virtue: Public school leadership in America 1920–1980. New York: Basic Books.

Wallace Foundation. 2013. The school principal as leader: Guiding schools to better teaching and learning. New York: Wallace Foundation.

Wideen, M., J. Mayer-Smith, and B. Moon. 1998. A critical analysis of the research on learning to teach: Making the case for an ecological perspective on inquiry. Review of Educational Research 68, no. 2: 130–78.

Wilmore, E. 2002. Principal leadership: Applying the new Educational Leadership Constituent Council (ELCC) standards. Thousand Oaks, CA: Corwin Press.

Yerkes, D. M., and C. L. Guaglianone. 1998. Where have all the high school administrators gone? Thrust for Educational Leadership 28, no. 2: 10–14.

Chapter One

Charter School Blues

Texas Principal Exam Competency 001: The principal knows how to shape campus culture by facilitating the development, articulation, implementation, and stewardship of a vision of learning that is shared and supported by the school community.

Texas Chapter 149 Standard 4 (2014): The principal is responsible for establishing and implementing a shared vision and culture of high expectations for all staff and students.

ELCC Standard 1.0 (2011): A building-level education leader applies knowledge that promotes the success of every student by collaboratively facilitating the development, articulation, implementation, and stewardship of a shared school vision of learning through the collection and use of data to identify school goals, assess organizational effectiveness, and implement school plans to achieve school goals; promotion of continual and sustainable school improvement; and evaluation of school progress and revision of school plans supported by school-based stakeholders.

ELCC Standard 2.0 (2011): A building-level education leader applies knowledge that promotes the success of every student by sustaining a school culture and instructional program conducive to student learning through collaboration, trust, and a personalized learning environment with high expectations for students; creating and evaluating a comprehensive, rigorous, and coherent curricular and instructional school program; developing and supervising the instructional and leadership capacity of school staff; and promoting the most effective and appropriate technologies to support teaching and learning within a school environment.

ABSTRACT

Two community charter schools have been closed by the state commissioner of education because the three hundred students at these schools were not meeting state academic standards. The local elementary school already has high enrollment and has not made plans to accommodate these children. The local high school has just achieved exemplary status and administrators are concerned that the influx of these low-performing students will cause the school to lose its hard-earned, prestigious ranking.

OBJECTIVES

1. The principal demonstrates a vision of learning that promotes the success of all students.
2. The principal uses strategies for involving all stakeholders in planning processes to enable the collaborative development of a shared campus vision focused on teaching and learning.
3. The principal responds appropriately to diverse needs in shaping the campus culture.
4. The principal creates a campus culture that sets high expectations, promotes learning, and provides intellectual stimulation for self, students, and staff.
5. The principal understands and promotes continual and sustainable school improvement.
6. The principal facilitates the collaborative development of a plan that clearly articulates objectives and strategies for implementing a campus vision.

LITERATURE REVIEW

Principals themselves have a strong influence on student learning (Fuller, Young, Barnett, Hirsch, and Byrd 2007; Leithwood, Day, Sammons, Hopkins, and Harris 2006; O'Donnell and White 2005). Thirty years ago, Robinson (1985) reported that effective schools have principals who do the following:

• Are assertive as instructional leaders
• Are goal and task oriented

- Are well organized and skilled in delegating responsibility to others
- Communicate high expectations for students as well as staff
- Define and communicate school policies clearly
- Are frequently seen in classrooms
- Are highly visible and available to faculty and staff
- Support the teaching staff
- Create good relationships with parents and the community

Nearly twenty years ago Hallinger and Heck (1996) determined that successful principals focused on influencing school processes directly linked to student learning, such as school policies, academic expectations, school mission, student learning, instruction, academic learning time, and the practice of teaching itself. Waters, Marzano, and McNulty (2003) confirmed through their meta-analysis a correlation of .25 between leadership and student achievement.

Fullan (2004) acknowledged that as society becomes more complex leadership must also become more sophisticated. Thus, Leithwood and Jantzi (2006) demonstrated that setting direction, helping individual teachers, fostering collaboration, and providing appropriate management and support are critical to aligning values that support student achievement. In addition, Kouzes and Posner (2007) noted that leaders must develop four key characteristics: honest, visionary, inspiring, and competent. More recently, Mullen and Robertson (2014) emphasized the importance of educating for critical consciousness in preparing school leaders to transform organizations.

Creating and Maintaining School Culture/Climate

Organizational culture and climate capture the atmosphere of schools. School culture is the "shared set of beliefs and values that binds the organization together and gives it a distinctive identity" (Hoy and Hoy 2003, 309). While climate "can be considered a manifestation of culture," it refers to patterns of behavior within the organization (Hoy and Hoy 2003, 282).

Matthews and Crow (2003) suggested that to maintain a perceived successful school culture, principals need to involve three groups of stakeholders: internal veterans, internal newcomers, and external constituents. Veteran faculty should be encouraged to continue what has worked in the past and are reminded by ceremonies and stories that reinforce the basic values of the school. Newcomers more easily maintain a school culture when they come to the school with similar values and beliefs as well as when a socializing process is available to communicate the prevailing norms and values. External constituents are those individuals and groups outside the school but connected to it. A major challenge of the principal is to communicate the values and beliefs of the school's culture to these stakeholders in order to gain their support of the school. Yet the principal must listen to their concerns and actively involve them in school planning and activities.

Most principals rarely have the opportunity to actually create a campus culture, instead they "inherit an existing culture" (Harris 2006, 38). Consequently, they must understand the existing culture and climate of the school in order to decide what needs to be nurtured, maintained, or revised. However, it is important to remember that change is necessary in all organizations. Thus, leader behavior that emphasizes trust is necessary to support the organization in moving forward with a positive organizational culture. Bryk and Schneider (2002) indicated that a school culture of trust is a strong predictor of student achievement more so than even socioeconomic status. In fact, Combs, Edmonson, and Harris (2013) suggested that a culture of trust makes the difference between leaders who succeed and leaders who do not.

Visionary Leadership

Effective principals have a personal vision that is focused on "improving teaching and learning for all students . . . and provides the passion for one activity over another" (Matthews and Crow 2003, 151). Starratt (1993) eloquently identified the vision as "a call to greatness" (145). According to Daft (1999), effective visions have five common themes:

- The vision is not the leader's alone but has broad appeal.
- The vision challenges people to make important changes toward improvement.
- The vision encourages people that they can be effective and gives them hope.
- The vision inspires and energizes people.
- The vision identifies specific outcomes for the school to achieve.

At the same time, principals must also work with faculty and other stakeholders to develop a collective or shared vision for the school. This is done by sharing and expressing personal visions among the different school groups. It is the principal's challenge to understand the differing visions of the school community and "find common ground that binds these personal visions into a collective vision for the school" (Matthews and Crow 2003, 152).

Developing a collective vision for the school takes time—it does not happen overnight. It involves commitment on the part of the principal to structure effective meetings and to find time for this to be a priority. Before strategic planning can be successful, there must be a shared vision on which to build. Principal Kathleen Haworth (in Harris 2006) emphasized the importance of the school vision in the process of strategic planning. Haworth pointed out that having a strategic planning team whose members are in agreement regarding the vision of the school is difficult, but it allows stakeholders to support the direction in which the school is moving. Thus sharing a common vision is integral to collaborative efforts to build and sustain school improvement.

Communicating the Vision

There are many ways for the school and community to partner together in collaboration, but communication is at the center of this effort (Harris 2006). In fact, open communication is one of the most important traits that effective schools have in common (Verdugo and Schneider 1999). Consequently, the principal must communicate the vision of the school to internal constituents, such as students and faculty, but it is equally important to involve individuals in the community outside the school. This necessitates that the principal become actively involved in the larger community and be aware of the changes and needs that are occurring. Effectively communicating the vision of the school at meetings and in publications encourages commitment throughout the different levels of the organization and the larger community. It facilitates decision making, setting priorities, and building relationships as people work together to create a school in which they have a personal interest and where they believe in the work being done.

CASE STUDY

State Education Agency Press Release

State Capital—Commissioner Dr. Emily Bronson orders shut down of two academically unacceptable charters in Greene. The schools, Academy Charter School and Valley High Charter School, will be closed at the end of the school year.

Each of the schools received an academically unacceptable rating for the past three years. These are the lowest ratings in the state's school accountability system. State law authorizes the commissioner to order closure of a campus that has been rated low performing for two or more years.

Bronson said, "Most charter schools are providing a sound education, but these two schools have a long record of unsatisfactory performance. It is not in the best interests of students to allow these schools to continue to operate. Research has shown that children who experience bad teaching have a hard time recovering. We need to help these children be successful in school."

Academy Charter School opened in September 2010 and had an enrollment of 228 students last year in grades prekindergarten through five. Valley High Charter School opened in October 2010 and served eighty-eight high school students last year.

Dr. Bronson said the students could return to Greene ISD (Independent School District) schools, enroll in a charter school in another town, home school, or seek admission to a private school.

Greene Elementary School

The press release from the State Education Agency confirmed that State Commissioner of Education, Dr. Emily Bronson, had ordered both Greene charter schools closed at the end of the school year. While there had been rumors that both Academy Charter School and Valley High Charter School were not meeting state academic standards, the article described both schools as academically unacceptable.

Greene Elementary School principal Lisa Billings read the press release carefully. She and her faculty had heard rumors that the school would be closing, but they had not begun any planning for serving the more than two hundred elementary students from Academy Charter School who would enroll at Greene Elementary School in the fall. She realized that some of these students would not want to come to Greene Elementary School and that many of their parents were very disappointed in the decision of the state commissioner to close the charter school. Since there was no other charter school in Greene, some parents would probably choose home schooling, but Lisa believed that a significant number of the charter school students would come to Greene Elementary.

Greene Elementary School already had high enrollment in all its classes because of the growing community in which the school was located. But of even greater concern to Principal Billings was that it seemed likely that many of the students coming from Academy Charter School would be behind academically, given their performance on state assessments in language arts, mathematics, social studies, and science.

Greene High School

Greene High School principal Terrence Simmons had already planned a meeting of the Campus Improvement Committee for tomorrow afternoon when he read the State Education Agency press release. Talk around town for the last several weeks that Valley High Charter School was in trouble was now confirmed. Valley High Charter School principal Debra Whitmire had written a letter to the editor of the *Greene Gazette* that had been published in last Sunday's edition. In her letter, Ms. Whitmire had harsh words about the State Education Agency:

> They don't want us to succeed. They don't give us enough money to hire experienced, certified teachers, and yet they hold us to the same standards as traditional public schools. Many of our students are at risk and are potential dropouts. They need a specialized program such as ours. They'll get lost again in the public school.

Since the academic performance of each school in the state was available on the State Education Agency's website, Principal Simmons had already studied Valley High Charter School's State Assessment of Academic Skills (SAAS) language arts and mathematics scores. Fewer than 50 percent of students had passed the SAAS last year.

Under Mr. Simmons's leadership, the Greene High School faculty had worked hard for the past five years developing a high school that promoted success for all students. Then Greene High School earned an exemplary rating, the state's highest academic ranking. Students were enrolling in more challenging courses, college entrance examination scores were higher than ever, and there was a spirit of success. Implementing the school's vision with collegiality and teamwork, using data-driven research strategies and best practices in classrooms, and involving community members in the realization of the vision was paying off.

How would the Valley High Charter School students fit into Greene High School? During his years with the Greene ISD, Mr. Simmons had worked with many of the charter school students (or at least knew their families), and he knew that most would not be pleased to return to Greene High. He also realized that they had few other options, there being no other charter school or private school in Greene. In fact, many of the poorest-performing students might even choose to drop out of school altogether.

DISCUSSION

1. Develop a vision statement for each school Greene Elementary School and Greene High School.
2. How will stakeholders be involved in the development of the vision statement?
3. On the basis of the vision statement, create campus plans that address curriculum, instruction, assessments, staff development, budgets, and resources.
4. What communication strategies will you use to sustain and nurture the school vision?
5. Will charter school students be assigned to classes according to chronological age? Should they be pretested to determine academic placement? How will you handle grade placement?
6. What strategies will you implement to ensure the academic success of all groups within the schools?
7. Identify obstacles that could inhibit effective communication with students, parents, faculty, and the community.
8. What will you do to change the negative perceptions of the former charter school students and parents about your school?
9. How will you motivate teachers and students already at the elementary and high school to accept these new students?
10. How will you address the issue of needed changes?

ON YOUR OWN—CONSIDER

Homelessness among public high school students is growing in your urban community. In fact, it is at an all-time high. Generally, these students drop out rather than struggle to stay in school. Some of the teenagers are homeless with their families, but others are simply on their own. No one is looking out for their well-being. As a public school, your school is required under federal law to ensure homeless students have access to a free public education.

In addition, your school must provide transportation. Teachers are concerned because of the lack of resources they have for everyone, let alone for the homeless students. Then there is the concern of lack of resources for these students—shelter, food, clothing, school needs, and other immediate needs.

You are the principal. What can you do to encourage these students to stay in school?

REMEMBER

The principal shapes campus culture by facilitating the development, articulation, implementation, and stewardship of a vision of learning that is shared and supported by the school community.

REFERENCES

Bryk, A. S., and B. Schneider. 2002. Trust in schools: A core resource for improvement. New York: Russell Sage Foundation.

Combs, J., S. Edmonson, and S. Harris. 2013. The trust factor. New York: Routledge.

Daft, R. 1999. Leadership theory and practice. Fort Worth, TX: Dryden.

Fullan, M. 2004. Leading in a culture of change: Personal action guide and workbook. San Francisco: Jossey-Bass.

Fuller, E., M. Young, B. Barnett, E. Hirsch, and A. Byrd. 2007. Examining school leadership behavior. Paper presented at the annual conference of the 2007 UCEA, Alexandria, VA.

Hallinger, P., and R. Heck. 1996. Reassessing the principal's role in school effectiveness: A review of empirical research, 1980–1995. Education Administration Quarterly 32, no. 3: 5–44.

Harris, S. 2006. Best practices of award-winning secondary school principals. Thousand Oaks, CA: Corwin Press.

Hoy, A., and W. Hoy. 2003. Instructional leadership: A learning-centered guide. Boston: Allyn & Bacon.

Kouzes, J. M., and B. Z. Posner. 2007. The leadership challenge. 4th ed. San Francisco: Wiley & Sons.

Leithwood, K., and D. Jantzi. 2006. Linking leadership to student learning: The contributions of leader efficacy. Toronto, CA: Ontario Institute of Studies in Education.

Leithwood, K., C. Day, P. Sammons, D. Hopkins, and A. Harris. 2006, March 30. Successful school leadership: What it is and how it influences student learning. Toronto, CA: Report to the Department for Education and Skills.

Matthews, L., and G. Crow. 2003. Being and becoming a principal: Role conceptions for contemporary principals and assistant principals. Boston: Allyn & Bacon.

Mullen, C. A., and K. C. Robertson. 2014. Shifting to fit: The politics of black and white identity in school leadership. Charlotte, NC: Information Age.

O'Donnell, R., and G. White. 2005. Within the accountability era: Principals' instructional leadership behaviors and student achievement. NASSP Bulletin 89, no. 745: 56–71.

Robinson, G. E. 1985. Effective schools research: A guide to school improvement. Arlington, VA: Educational Research Service.

Starratt, R. 1993. The drama of leadership. London: Falmer Press.

Verdugo, R., and J. Schneider. 1999. Quality schools, safe schools: A theoretical and empirical discussion. Education & Urban Society 31: 286–308.

Waters, T., R. J. Marzano, and B. McNulty. 2003. Balanced leadership: What 30 years of research tells us about the effect of leadership on student achievement. Denver, CO: McREL.

ADDITIONAL RESOURCES

Blanchard, K., and S. Bowles. 1998. Gung-ho! New York: William Morrow.

Bolman, L., and T. Deal. 2001. Leading with soul: An uncommon journey of spirit. San Francisco: Jossey-Bass.

DePree, M. 1989. Leadership is an art. New York: Dell.

Fullan, M. 2001. Leading in a culture of change. San Francisco: Jossey-Bass.

Harris, S. 2009. Learning from the best: Lessons from award-winning superintendents. Thousand Oaks, CA: Corwin Press.

Hoyle, J. 1995. Leadership and futuring: Making visions happen. Thousand Oaks, CA: Corwin Press.

Hoyle, J. 2001. Leadership and the force of love: Six keys to motivating with love. Thousand Oaks, CA: Corwin Press.

Kouzes, J., and B. Posner. 1998. Encouraging the heart: A leader's guide to rewarding and recognizing others. San Francisco: Jossey-Bass.

Nanus, B. 1992. Visionary leadership: Creating a compelling sense of direction for your organization. San Francisco: Jossey-Bass.

Schein, E. 1992. Organizational culture and leadership. 2nd ed. San Francisco: Jossey-Bass.

Senge, P. 1990. The fifth discipline: The art and practice of the learning organization. New York: Doubleday.

Chapter Two

Who Is in Charge Here

Texas Principal Exam Competency 002: The principal knows how to communicate and collaborate with all members of the school community, respond to diverse interests and needs, and mobilize resources to promote student success.

Texas Chapter 149 Standard 2 (2014): Human Capital. The principal is responsible for ensuring there are high-quality teachers and staff in every classroom and throughout the school.

Texas Chapter 149 Standard 3 (2014): Executive Leadership. The principal is responsible for modeling a consistent focus on and commitment to improving student learning.

ELCC Standard 4.0 (2011): A building-level education leader applies knowledge that promotes the success of every student by collaborating with faculty and community members, responding to diverse community interests and needs, and mobilizing community resources on behalf of the school by collecting and analyzing information pertinent to improvement of the school's educational environment; promoting an understanding, appreciation, and use of the diverse cultural, social, and intellectual resources within the school community; building and sustaining positive school relationships with families and caregivers; and cultivating productive school relationships with community partners.

ABSTRACT

Both case studies in this chapter involve principals at the center of conflict. Case Study 1 is a low-performing school with a very diverse population and a new principal. Much of the conflict appears to center on just how much parental involvement is appropriate. Case Study 2 is a school with a veteran principal, and the conflict reflects the changing times and the problems that can arise as a result.

OBJECTIVES

1. The principal collaborates with faculty and community members by collecting and analyzing information pertinent to the improvement of the school's educational environment.
2. The principal understands and can mobilize community resources by promoting an understanding, appreciation, and use of diverse cultural, social, and intellectual resources within the school community.
3. The principal understands and can respond to community interests and needs by building and sustaining positive school relationships with families and caregivers.

LITERATURE REVIEW

Creating Collaborative Schools as Learning Communities

Learning the value of collaboration is important because principals, faculty, and community stakeholders must work together to further school goals and objectives. In fact, Ramsey (2005) suggested that for principals to succeed in the twenty-first century, faculty and staff must include community stakeholders for an array of supports, such as resources, volunteers, discipline, ideas, advocacy, money, and many more. Nearly twenty-five years ago, Sergiovanni (1992) argued that principals who are responsive to the norms of school as learning communities provide teachers and other adults who work in and for schools with inspiration and motivation that are internal rather than in exchange for something.

Traditionally, schools have been organized under instructional delivery systems that are management and leadership intensive. Schools organized as learning communities, instead, are concerned with relationships among parents, students, teachers, administrators, and even community stakeholders and how they can work together. Learning-community schools are concerned that the community is bonded through shared values, purposes, and commitments.

Sergiovanni (1992) emphasized that as schools become more a community, the practice of teaching becomes transformed from an individual to a collective issue. Thus, the principal's role becomes less that of manager intent on controlling, organizing, and leading and more one of "supporter, reinforcer, and facilitator" (50). As collegiality and collaboration become the norm on campuses, the principal's leadership changes from one of providing direct "interpersonal leadership" to providing encouragement for "others to be leaders" (98).

DuFour and Mattos (2013) emphasized that principals who want to improve student achievement should not focus on the individual inspection of teaching, but instead, "focus on the collective analysis of evidence of student learning" (36). Thus, administrators are responsible for establishing an environment where faculty and staff communicate, share a common vision of learning, and exhibit a level of cohesion between the team members.

As DuFour (2004) noted, professional learning communities (PLCs) provide a sense of collaboration and creative thinking as teams of teachers work and communicate together ways to improve student learning. The focus of the PLC is to increase awareness of all individuals involved so they can communicate ideas and focus on instruction. DuFour posed three critical questions on which professional learning communities should focus. These include the following:

1. What do we want each student to learn?
2. How will we know when each student has learned it?
3. How will we respond when a student experiences difficulty in learning? (1)

The principal must focus the group's efforts on these three questions and ensure the focus and vision of the group remains set on improving student success in the classroom. As long as student success is the focus, faculty and staff will continue to collaborate and work together to find new ways to deliver instruction to improve student success.

DuFour and Marzano (2011) argued that administrators are responsible to create an environment where faculty, staff, and community stakeholders focus on a shared vision and a culture that supports collaboration. The principal must know what the classroom instruction looks like. Principals must be able to gauge the level of instruction within classrooms and then be able to determine if the learning community is increasing the level of instruction over time.

Administrators lead the charge in setting specific goals for faculty and staff to meet and follow as they collaborate with each other. There are strategies that principals need to consider when establishing PLCs on a campus. For example, McDonough (2013) noted the importance of setting aside common planning times for teachers to collaborate and plan. In addition, the establishment of a PLC is based on building trusting relationships with fellow teachers. When an effective PLC is established, teachers felt supported, and new teaching techniques and intervention strategies were identified, strengthened, and implemented in the classroom.

Shared Decision Making

A key ingredient of successful collaboration is shared decision making. Jackson (2001) recommended a model for shared decision making for principals to follow called the Politically Competent Decision-Making Model (PCDMM). While the PCDMM is similar to traditional decision-making models, it pays special attention to the need to minimize negative effects on the organizational climate and does this through involving a broad base of stakeholders in the process. This model includes the following six steps:

1. Identify the problem—then determine which individuals can inform the decision-making process, such as students, parents, faculty, and other community resource people.
2. Verify that the problem actually exists in the perception of the majority of the organization or community—then involve appropriate people to explore solutions.
3. Develop alternatives for solutions—then reconsider who should provide input in order to involve appropriate individuals to gather the best information.
4. Evaluate alternatives through the lens of the school's past history, parameters, policies, and processes.
5. Select and implement one of the alternatives—then, once again, select and involve appropriate input sources.

6. Evaluate the effects of the decision regularly while monitoring the changes in the environment.

Changing Demographics

Schools are increasingly becoming places where cultural issues are brought to the forefront each day (Harris and Jenkins 2013). According to Cauchon and Overberg (2012), the U.S. Census Bureau reported in 2011 that Hispanics, African Americans, Asians, and other minority populations accounted for over 50 percent of births and 49.7 percent of all children under five in the United States. Other demographic changes are occurring in the United States as well. English, Papa, Mullen, and Creighton (2012) reported that poverty is a growing concern with rates for African Americans at 25.8 percent and for Hispanics at 25.3 percent. In fact, children are 25 percent of the total population of the nation, yet they represent 35 percent of the poor.

An effective way for schools to respond to student diversity issues is to implement collaborative strategies for joint problem solving. Harris and Jenkins (2013) used the analogy of a cultural highway model in which all stakeholders are engaged. This model begins with cultural deficit, cultural denial, cultural discovery, cultural celebration, cultural conscience, and hopefully ends the journal at cultural community. Harris and Jenkins provided a framework for analyzing cultural conflict (FACC) that implements four steps:

- identify the nature of the cultural conflict;
- consider the choices available and possible consequences of the choices;
- implement an appropriate conflict management strategy;
- commit to continuing on the cultural journey with training as a community of learners. (14)

Therefore, it is a responsibility of the principal to create vehicles that lead to staff members' growth, such as involving faculty members in study groups. Typically, faculty members involved in reflection and focused study groups indicate an increased interest and openness in solving school problems that result in serving students better. Because of changing demographics, the growing diversity of communities, and other external influences, leaders are faced with challenges that must include an understanding of the larger community.

Parent Involvement

Research overwhelmingly demonstrates that parent involvement is positively related to student achievement in schools (Barnard 2004; Henderson and Map 2002; Smith, Wohlstetter, Kuzin, and De Pedro 2011). Results that are noticeable include students staying in school longer, an increase in grades, attendance, state test results, and a more positive outlook on school including a better attitude and higher personal expectations (Henderson and Map 2002; Smith, Wohlstetter, Kuzin, and De Pedro 2011).

Parental involvement has the greatest influence when parents know what is happening at the school their children attend and when educators openly seek input from the communities from which the children come (Orozco 2008). Silver (2005) found that when parents are involved, students achieve more, regardless of socioeconomic status, ethnic/racial background, or parent education level. When parents are involved, students exhibit more positive attitudes and behavior. In addition, children from diverse cultural backgrounds tend to do better when parents and professionals collaborate to bridge the gap between the culture, the home, and the learning institution. In addition, Pape (1999) found that schools that have good relationships with families have improved teacher morale and teachers are rated higher by parents.

Unfortunately, parent participation of limited-English-proficient (LEP) students in school is often low. Yet Hinojosa (2013) found that elements that contributed to positive school experiences for Hispanic students occurred when parents perceived that students had caring teachers, and when the school personnel recognized their student's personal determination. Hinojosa also found that Hispanic parents who feel welcome in the school consider their cultural and language barriers as minimized. These adults also have an increased respect and admiration for school personnel.

CASE STUDY 1

West Oak Elementary School was struggling academically, with state assessment scores barely at the satisfactory level. In addition, there were serious gaps between the test scores of the predominantly low socioeconomic Hispanic students and the more affluent white students. Compared to the eight other elementary schools in the Clarkton Independent School District, West Oak Elementary was barely passing.

When Matilde Cordova was named principal of West Oak Elementary School last year, she knew that an increased level of parental involvement at the school was one of the first things that she and her faculty would address. As the first in her family to complete a college degree, she knew firsthand the importance of family involvement and support of education. Just as her parents had encouraged and supported their children, Matilde felt strongly that the parents wanted the same good education and chances for success for their children that her parents had wanted—they just needed opportunities for participation at the school. In their early planning sessions, she and the team leaders agreed that parental involvement was necessary if the 528 West Oak Elementary School students were to excel. As the first Spanish-speaking principal of West Oak Elementary School, she was certain that she could and would effectively communicate with parents to accomplish this goal.

Ms. Cordova and the team leaders had implemented an aggressive plan to increase parental involvement. They met with small groups of parents, visited neighborhood churches, and worked with the existing Parent-Teacher Organization (PTO) and site-based decision-making committees to encourage parents to participate in a number of roles. Matilde had personally organized after-school tutorials for LEP students, with parents serving as volunteer tutors. The after-school tutorial program was now serving almost every LEP student at West Oak Elementary School. Many of the parents who had been reluctant at first were now enthusiastic about working with students.

Today, Suzanne Garrison, a veteran fifth-grade teacher and chair of the Campus Improvement Committee, had come to Ms. Cordova with concerns about the after-school tutoring program. Ms. Garrison had come right to the point and complained that "those parents are taking over and trying to run things." Apparently, several teachers shared this sentiment, and Ms. Garrison had been appointed the unofficial spokesperson for a group of teachers who were thinking that while some parental involvement was probably all right, this particular project had gone too far. She said, "They're wanting to make curriculum decisions and tell us how to teach. Remember, not one of those parents ever finished high school. We're the professionals here, and they've gone too far!"

Early the next morning, Marisela Gutierrez, mother of two West Oak Elementary School students and a very active parent volunteer, had called Ms. Cordova to say that she would no longer be helping with the after-school tutoring program. According to Ms. Gutierrez, Ms. Garrison had "told her off" and let her know that her help was not needed.

CASE STUDY 2

As far back as anyone could remember, the PTO of Byers Elementary School had sponsored a Halloween Carnival on the Friday night before Halloween. Students came in costume. Parent volunteers and faculty worked together in such booths as the fish pond, bingo, costume contest, dunking for apples, and spin-the-wheel. The school gymnasium was always lavishly decorated, and it had become a neighborhood event as well as a school activity. In fact, Gayle Edwards, a retired teacher and neighborhood resident, was one of several retirees and neighborhood residents who volunteered their time at the carnival.

Larry Wagner had been principal of Byers Elementary School for fourteen years, and he had never heard anything negative about the Halloween Carnival. But then last year several parents had voiced concerns that the Halloween decorations, including witches and goblins, were inappropriate and unsuitable for elementary children. One parent had been especially concerned that the school was promoting devil worship.

As he listened to the PTO officers describing the changes they had in mind for the Halloween Carnival, Mr. Wagner was dismayed. Two of the PTO leaders, Cynthia Wilson and Betty Van Hook, were especially vocal that the school should no longer sponsor an anti-Christian activity. They contended that the Halloween Carnival should be changed to a Harvest Festival, no costumes should be allowed, and absolutely no games of chance, such as bingo, should be permitted. The fact that many teachers and school staff members wore costumes themselves was considered highly inappropriate by these parents.

Mr. Wagner was not sure whether these two mothers, Ms. Wilson and Ms. Van Hook, were speaking on behalf of the entire PTO, but they certainly seemed to be in charge of the PTO officers today.

DISCUSSION

1. What information about the larger communities of these schools would be helpful in bringing about a solution?
2. How would implementing PLCs in both of these schools make a difference in addressing these cases?
3. Design a plan for the school in case 1 that will improve relationships between parents and school faculty.

4. What advice would you give the new principal in case 1 that might have prevented this problem?

5. Design a plan for the school in case 2 that will bring about an effective solution.

6. In working toward more collaborative school environments, what stakeholders would you recommend be involved in each step of decision making for these cases?

7. What suggestions would you make to the veteran principal in case 2 that might avoid this type of problem in the future?

8. Consider your school. What steps would you follow to make it more collaborative?

9. Survey stakeholders in your community about how collaborative they consider your school. What suggestions would they make for it to become more collaborative?

10. Design a plan for your school to identify and support students from a different cultural background.

11. Are activities such as the Halloween party in case 2 appropriate? Defend your response.

ON YOUR OWN—CONSIDER

A Southern community was experiencing many demographic changes. Some of this was attributed to migrant workers who were taking up residence. For years, migrant workers had come to this city, but their children were rarely enrolled in school, and after the growing season was over, the families left the city. In addition, Hindu families were settling into the community and working in low-wage jobs. The discontent in the high school was obvious. The Hispanic students, the Hindu students, the black students, and the white students were segregating into four distinct groups.

Soon after school was dismissed on October 15, students left the building and moved into four groups. They began yelling and taunting one another and throwing rocks. After about ten minutes, the police arrived and the groups dispersed. The principal of the high school was met at his office the following morning by a group of angry, primarily white, parents who insisted that the school expel the offending groups; after all, these students "just do not belong at our school." Teachers were upset. As one teacher commented, "We can't teach with such discontent among the students."

You are the principal . . . what will you do to bring resolution?

REMEMBER

The principal communicates and collaborates with all stakeholders, responds to diverse student populations, and mobilizes resources to promote student success.

REFERENCES

Barnard, W. M. 2004. Parent involvement in elementary school and educational attainment. Children and Youth Services Review 26, no. 1: 39–62. doi:10.1016/j.childyouth .2003.11.002.

Cauchon, D., and P. Overberg. 2012, May 17. Minorities are now a majority of births. USA Today, 1A.

DuFour, R. 2004. What is a "professional learning community"? Schools as Learning Communities 61, no. 8: 6–11.

DuFour, R., and Marzano, R. J. 2011. Leaders of learning: How district, school, and classroom leaders improve student achievement. Bloomington, IN: Solution Tree Press.

DuFour, R. and M. Mattos. 2013. How do principals really improve schools? Educational Leadership 70, no. 1: 34–40.

English, F.W., R. Papa, C. A. Mullen, and T. Creighton. 2012. Educational leadership at 2050. Lanham, MD: Rowman & Littlefield.

Harris, S., and S. Jenkins. 2013. Conflicts in culture: Strategies to understand and resolve the issues. Lanham, MD: Rowman & Littlefield.

Henderson, A., and K. Mapp. 2002. A new wave of evidence: The impact of school, family and community connections on student achievement. Austin, TX: Southwest Educational Development Laboratory.

Hinojosa, H. 2013. Parental influences and effective school practices that contribute to first and second generation Latino student success: A phenomenological study. Unpublished doctoral dissertation. Beaumont, TX: Lamar University.

Jackson, J. 2001. Politically competent decision making. Principal Leadership 2, no. 4: 25–28.

McDonough, J. 2013. A case study of how professional learning communities influence morale and rigor in the classroom. Unpublished doctoral dissertation. Beaumont, TX: Lamar University.

Orozco, G. 2008. Understanding the culture of low-income immigrant Latino parents: Key to involvement. School Community Journal 18, no. 1: 21–37.

Pape, B. 1999. Involving parents lets students and teachers win. Education Digest 64, no. 6: 47–51.

Ramsey, R. D. 2005. What matters most for school leaders. Thousand Oaks, CA: Corwin Press.

Rosenthal, D., and J. Sawyers. 1996. Building successful home/school partnerships. Childhood Education 72, no. 4: 194–200.

Sergiovanni, T. 1992. Moral leadership: Getting to the heart of school improvement. San Francisco: Jossey-Bass.

———. 2001. The principalship: A reflective practice perspective. 4th ed. Boston: Allyn & Bacon.

Silver, D. 2005. Drumming to the beat of different marchers. Nashville, TN: Incentive Publications.

Smith, J., P. Wohlstetter, C. Kuzin, and K. De Pedro, K. 2011. Parent involvement in urban charter schools: New strategies for increasing participation. School Community Journal 21, no. 1: 71–94. doi:10.1080/15582159.2011.624938.

ADDITIONAL RESOURCES

Boske, C. (ed.). 2012. Educational leadership: Building bridges among ideas, schools and nations. Charlotte, NC: Information Age.

Cordeiro, P. A., and W. G. Cunningham. Educational leadership: A bridge to improved practice. 5th ed. Boston: Pearson.

DePree, M. 1997. Leading without power: Finding hope in serving community. San Francisco: Jossey-Bass.

McCray, C. R., and F. D. Beachman. 2014. School leadership in a diverse society: Helping schools prepare all students for success. Charlotte, NC: Information Age.

Pellicer, L. 1999. Caring enough to lead: Schools and the sacred trust. Thousand Oaks, CA: Corwin Press.

Sergiovanni, T. 2000. The lifeworld of leadership: Creating culture, community and personal meaning in our schools. San Francisco: Jossey-Bass.

Chapter Three

Principals with Principles

Texas Principal Exam Competency 003: The principal knows how to act with integrity, fairness, and in an ethical and legal manner.

Texas Chapter 149 Standard 3 (2014): Executive Leadership. The principal is responsible for modeling a consistent focus on and commitment to improving student learning.

ELCC Standard 4 (2011): A building-level education leader applies knowledge that promotes the success of every student by collaborating with faculty and community members, responding to diverse community interests and needs, and mobilizing community resources on behalf of the school by collecting and analyzing information pertinent to improvement of the school's educational environment; promoting an understanding, appreciation, and use of the diverse cultural, social, and intellectual resources within the school community; building and sustaining positive school relationships with families and caregivers; and cultivating productive school relationships with community partners.

ELCC Standard 5 (2011): A building-level education leader applies knowledge that promotes the success of every student by acting with integrity, fairness, and in an ethical manner to ensure a school system of accountability for every student's academic and social success by modeling school principles of self-awareness, reflective practice, transparency, and ethical behavior as related to their roles within the school; safeguarding the values of democracy, equity, and diversity within the school; evaluating the potential moral and legal consequences of decision making in the school; and promoting social justice within the school to ensure that individual student needs inform all aspects of schooling.

ABSTRACT

One of the most complex issues facing principals today is that of making decisions that are ethical as well as equitable. In case 1, a principal is faced with a difficult decision that concerns the whole community and will create a strong emotional backlash. In case 2, the principal is faced with a personnel issue that will have long-term impact on the level of trust with faculty.

OBJECTIVES

1. The principal understands and can respond to community interests and needs by building and sustaining productive school relationships with community partners.
2. The principal understands and responds to community interests and needs by building and sustaining positive school relationships with families and caregivers.
3. The principal understands and acts with integrity and fairness to ensure that schools are accountable for every student's academic and social success
4. The principal understands and can safeguard the values of democracy, equity and diversity.

LITERATURE REVIEW

Hodgkinson (1991) asserted that "values, morals, and ethics are the very stuff of leadership" (11). In fact Sergiovanni (1991) argued that "every technical decision has moral implications" (42). Marshall and Kasten (1994) pointed out that, other than religion, no issue is as value laden as education; consequently, the conflict between the administrator's value system and handling problems that occur can be "tortuous" (12). Our increasingly diverse yet interdependent society looks at schooling and child rearing in a myriad of ways. Likewise, school policies are often the "result of political, value-laden choices," yet administrators must implement these policies, often in direct conflict with the desires of parents, faculty, and administrators themselves

(12). Nowhere is this conflict more obvious than in politically state-mandated testing and its effect on minority students.

Sergiovanni (1992) suggested that ethical leadership is comprised of three dimensions: the heart (personal values and beliefs), the head (knowledge), and the hand (actions). In the role of principal, it is not uncommon for incidents to arise that cause conflict among these three dimensions. In addition, Starratt (1994) developed an ethical model that focused on the ethic of care (actions must show that we care), the ethic of justice (actions that are equitable), and the ethic of critique (actions that facilitate deep dialogue to advocate for the powerless). In other words, legal or political factors may suggest that one course of action be taken, yet morally or ethically the principal feels that other actions would be best suited in a particular instance (Kowalski 2001).

Ethical Leadership

To be a leader is to live daily with ethical dilemmas and making decisions that uphold the structure, policy, and practice of the school while meeting the needs of people affected by those decisions (Starratt 1991). Therefore, principals are constantly faced with making decisions that are the "right thing," but the challenge lies in determining just what the right thing is (Arnold and Harris 2000, 12). Faculty members look to the principal regarding ethical decisions on their campus. Thus, an ethical leader-principal challenges faculty to think beyond strategies and their immediate effect and to develop and nurture moral growth in children.

A type of ethical leadership was proposed by Greenleaf (1977), who identified the servant leader as a servant whose goal is to make sure that individuals grow as people and become healthier, wiser, and freer. By meeting the needs of others first, servant leaders can then lead them in achieving those goals. The idea of transforming leadership was conceptualized by Burns (1978), who referred to transformational leadership as a relationship of shared vision and goals "that converts followers into leaders and leaders into moral agents" (4). Burns asserted that through transformational leadership, both leaders and followers raise their performance to higher levels of motivation and morality.

In continuing to develop the idea of moral leadership, Sergiovanni (1992) suggested the following beliefs for principals who would lead an ethical "virtuous school":

- The school must become a learning community.
- Every student can learn and does everything possible to see that every student does learn.
- Schools should provide for the whole student and the ethic of care is key to academic success.
- Respect for all is honored.
- Parents, teachers, community, and school are partners (112–13).

Ethical Decision Making

Because of the value conflict inherent in decision making, Sergiovanni (1992) suggested a guiding framework based on Frankena's (1973) work for deciding on moral principles that can guide administrative actions themselves: the principle of justice and the principle of beneficence. The principle of justice involves equal treatment and respect for each individual within the school community. The principle of beneficence is concern for the welfare of the school as a community and the understanding that each action of the school should advance community welfare.

Based on the guiding principles of justice and beneficence, Sergiovanni (1992) further recommended three tests for considering whether a norm, value, or purpose should be a part of a school's ethical covenant: Kant's (1959) "second categorical imperative," John Rawls's (1971) "veil of ignorance," and Habermas's (1990) "moment of empathy" (106).

Kant's (1959) second categorical imperative is that of acting so that all humanity is treated always as an end and never as a means only. Thus, the role of leadership would no longer be based on getting others to do what the leader wants; rather, the leader would exert influence based on the "substance of ideas, values, and commitment" (106). This would require greater openness and forthrightness among leaders than is typically the case.

Rawls's (1971) veil of ignorance asserts that "just principles are those that people choose in a hypothetical position of fairness while under a 'veil of ignorance'" (107). In other words, when we do not know anything about ourselves (race, sex, talents, or position), we make decisions that are fairer and more equitable without considering self-interest.

Habermas's (1990) moment of empathy involves putting oneself in the place of everyone else (parent, principal, student, teacher, or others) to discuss whether a "norm is fair enough for everyone to accept" (107). This allows leaders to better understand circumstances through the eyes of others.

Furman (2002) noted that for twenty-first-century leaders there is a shift from the historical model of leadership and the decision making that follows. Historically, the *leadership-about* model has been emphasized. But this has increasingly become a model of *leadership-for*. In the traditional leadership model, it was about who the leader is and what the leader does that guided decision making. But for the leader of today, leadership must be more focused on decisions guided by *leadership-for* (for social justice, for ethical schools, for democracy).

Yet, Hudak (2007), building on the work of Freire (1997), extended the model of ethical leadership even more by suggesting a model of leadership that emphasizes *leadership-with*. This model emphasizes an *intensity* of acting on one's commitment related to that of a revolutionary urgency to *stand with* (349) the community of learners to promote authentic learning for all.

Ethical Standards

National Association of Secondary School Principals adopted a code of ethics for school leaders in November, 1973, which was revised November 7, 2013. See textbox 3.1.

**Textbox 3.1. National Association of Secondary
School Principals: Ethical Standards**

Issue: School leaders—who are also leaders in their communities and models of leadership for teachers and students—must maintain standards of exemplary professional conduct.

Guiding Principles: NASSP supports the 2008 Educational Leadership Standards from the Council of Chief State School Officers that call for education leaders to promote the success of every student by acting with integrity, fairness, and in an ethical manner.

In addition, the NASSP position statement on Internet and Wireless Safety offers recommendations for school leaders who face the triple challenge of protecting their students against online predators while safeguarding students' First Amendment rights and encouraging the use of the Internet as a pedagogical tool.

RECOMMENDATIONS: THE SCHOOL LEADER

1. Makes the well-being and success of students the fundamental value in all decision making and actions.
2. Fulfills professional responsibilities with honesty and integrity.
3. Supports the principle of due process and protects the civil and human rights of all individuals.
4. Obeys local, state, and federal laws.
5. Implements the governing board of education's policies and administrative rules and regulations.
6. Pursues appropriate measures to correct those laws, policies, and regulations that are not consistent with sound educational goals.
7. Avoids using positions for personal gain through political, social, religious, economic, or other influence.
8. Accepts academic degrees or professional certification only from duly accredited institutions.
9. Maintains the standards of and seeks to improve the effectiveness of the profession through research and continuing professional development.
10. Honors all contracts until fulfillment, release, or dissolution mutually agreed upon by all parties to contract.

RESOURCES

Council of Chief State School Officers. 2008. Educational leadership policy standards: ISLLC 2008. Retrieved from www.ccsso.org/documents/2008/educational_leadership_policy_standards_2008.pdf.

National Association of Secondary School Principals (NASSP). 2010. Internet and wireless safety. (Position statement). Retrieved from www.nassp.org/Content.aspx?topic=55883.

Source: www.nassp.org.

The National Association of Elementary School Professionals (NAESP) has also adopted a code of ethics. See textbox 3.2.

Textbox 3.2. National Association of Elementary
School Professionals: Code of Ethics

An educational administrator's professional behavior must conform to an ethical code. The code must be idealistic and at the same time practical so that it can apply reasonably to all educational administrators. The administrator acknowledges that the schools belong to the public they serve for the purpose of providing educational opportunities to all. However, the administrator assumes responsibility for providing professional leadership in the school and community. This responsibility requires the administrator to maintain standards of exemplary professional conduct. It must be recognized that the administrator's actions will be viewed and appraised by the community, professional associates, and students. To these ends, the administrator subscribes to the following statements of standards. The educational administrator:

1. Makes the well-being of students the fundamental value in all decision making and actions.
2. Fulfills professional responsibilities with honesty and integrity.
3. Supports the principle of due process and protects the civil and human rights of all individuals.
4. Obeys local, state, and national laws and does not knowingly join or support organizations that advocate, directly or indirectly, the overthrow of the government.
5. Implements the governing board of education's policies and administrative rules and regulations.
6. Pursues appropriate measures to correct those laws, policies, and regulations that are not consistent with sound educational goals.
7. Avoids using positions for personal gain through political, social, religious, economic, or other influence.
8. Accepts academic degrees or professional certification only from duly accredited institutions.
9. Maintains the standards and seeks to improve the effectiveness of the profession through research and continuing professional development.
10. Honors all contracts until fulfillment or release.

Policy Statement 1100.2 Statement of Ethics for School Administrators
Adopted by the NAESP Board of Directors September 29, 1976.
Source: www.naesp.org.

Most states have adopted ethical standards for educators. What ethical standards are supported by your state?

CASE STUDY 1

The Brownville High School football team was on its way to the regional play-offs next week. Their spot in the play-offs was already in place, and tonight's victory over neighboring Augusta High School was just icing on the cake. A community pep rally and parade tomorrow morning in downtown Brownville was sure to be well attended—just another indicator of the interest and pride that residents of the Brownville Integrated School District had in this team.

The Brownville High School Wildcats, coached by longtime head coach Warren Adams, had a 7–1 record, and football fever was high. Coach Adams had been quoted earlier in the season in the town's daily newspaper, the *Brownville Gazette*: "This is the best group of athletes I've ever coached. If we don't have injuries and the kids keep up their grades, we're well positioned to win the state championship." But now it seemed that injuries and grades would not be the determining factors. The arrest of senior student and star running back Christopher Swope last week had shaken other Brownville High School students, his fellow football players, the coaching staff, and the entire community. Last night's victory had only momentarily focused attention away from Christopher's dilemma.

Today, high school principal Mary Ann Dillon sat in her office with Coach Adams; Christopher's parents, Carl and Jessie Swope; and their attorney, Robert Lawrence. Dillon had just been told that Christopher was being released from the county jail on bail later this afternoon. Eighteen-year-old Christopher had been charged and arrested as an adult in the alleged robbery of a convenience store in the nearby community of Brookstone. Two juveniles had been charged and arrested in the robbery also, but because of their ages, their cases had been handled by the juvenile justice system. Legally, Christopher was an adult.

Coach Adams had decided that Christopher would be allowed to play football next Friday night in the regional play-off game against the Whitefield Bulldogs. Mr. and Mrs. Swope were supporting that decision. Mr. Swope announced, "Christopher made a mistake, but he's been preparing for this game since he started football in the seventh grade. Now this is his senior year, and this is his big chance. The team needs him, and he needs to come back." Their attorney, Robert Lawrence, was quoting a similar case in another state. Ms. Dillon listened carefully because she knew that her decision would affect many lives.

CASE STUDY 2

Debra Pennington, principal of Weldon Elementary School, faced a tearful and very upset teacher. When second-grade teacher Nancy Musick told Ms. Pennington last week that she would be out for several weeks, beginning a chemotherapy regime for breast cancer, Nancy had assumed that the conversation would be confidential. However, yesterday afternoon at the local supermarket, another Weldon Elementary School teacher, Paula Carter, shared her concerns about Nancy's health and wished her a full recovery. Since Nancy had told only one person, her principal, about her medical condition, she knew that Debra had not kept their conversation private.

Indeed, Debra had discussed Nancy's cancer diagnosis and treatment with two other second-grade teachers soon after Nancy left her office last Wednesday afternoon. They had considered plans for a substitute teacher to teach in Nancy's absence and whether to tell the second-graders about the seriousness of Nancy's illness.

Now Nancy is very upset, charging Debra with betraying a confidence. Nancy said, "If I had wanted the entire school to know, I would have told them myself. I trusted you to help me, and you let me down."

DISCUSSION

1. Using ethical decision-making guidelines, what steps would you follow to decide whether the athlete in case 1 should play?
2. How would you explain your decision to those involved?
3. What might some of the political implications be regarding your decision?
4. Role-play a conference with one of the stakeholders who disagrees with the decision you made as principal in case 1.

5. Can you justify the actions of the principal in case 2? Why or why not?
6. With a partner, role-play case 2 and how you would handle this conference if you were the principal.
7. Develop your personal code of ethics to use in professional situations.
8. Would your professional code of ethics differ from your personal code of ethics for your personal life? If so, in what ways? If not, why?
9. In small groups, discuss ethical dilemmas that you have dealt with in the past. Reflect on how you made your decision. Could you have improved on that decision? In what ways?
10. Find a copy of your state's educators' code of ethics. Compare it to the codes provided in this chapter.

ON YOUR OWN—CONSIDER

Mr. Johnson is a member of a very conservative church in the community. He has concerns with has daughter's homework assignment which was to write a paper about the Islamic religion in a world history class. He considers this an "un-American assignment." Last night he met with his daughter's teacher and asked that she be removed from the class while this topic was being covered and be excused from completing the assignment. The teacher refused to comply with this request and told him that his daughter would receive a zero on the assignment if it was not completed. He shouted this was, "Unfair," and left the meeting very angry. This morning, he is sitting outside the principal's office.

You are the principal. How will you respond to his concern?

REMEMBER

The principal knows how to act with integrity, fairness, and in an ethical and legal manner.

REFERENCES

Arnold, M., and S. Harris. 2000. The song sounds better when all the notes are there. Contemporary Education 71, no. 4: 12–15.
Burns, J. 1978. Leadership. New York: Harper & Row.
Frankena, W. K. 1973. Ethics. Englewood Cliffs, NJ: Prentice Hall.
Freire, P. 1997. Pedagogy of the oppressed. New York: Continuum.

Furman, G. 2003. Postmodernism and community in schools: Unraveling the paradox. In *School as community.* Edited by G. Furman. Albany, NY: SUNY Press.

Greenleaf, R. 1977. Servant leadership. New York: Paulist Press.

Habermas, J. 1990. Moral consciousness and communicative action. Translated by C. Lenhardt and S. W. Nicholsen. Cambridge, MA: MIT Press.

Hodgkinson, C. 1991. Educational leadership: The moral art. Albany, NY: State University of New York Press.

Hudak, G. 2007. Leadership with: A spiritual perspective on professional & revolutionary leadership in a digital culture. In *Keeping the promise* (335–56). Edited by D. Carlson and C. P. New York: Peter Lang.

Kant, I. 1959. Foundations of the metaphysics of minds. Translated by L. W. Beck. New York: Bobbs-Merrill.

Kowalski, T. 2001. Case studies on educational administration. 3rd ed. New York: Longman.

Marshall, C., and K. Kasten. 1994. The administrative career: A casebook on entry, equity, and endurance. Thousand Oaks, CA: Corwin Press.

Matthews, L., and G. Crow. 2003. Being and becoming a principal: Role conceptions for contemporary principals and assistant principals. Boston: Allyn & Bacon.

Rawls, J. 1971. A theory of justice. Cambridge, MA: Harvard University Press.

Sergiovanni, T. 1991. Constructing and changing theories of practice: The key to preparing school administrators. Urban Review 23, no. 1: 39–49.

———. 1992. Moral leadership: Getting to the heart of school improvement. San Francisco: Jossey-Bass.

Starratt, R. 1991. Building an ethical school: A theory for practice in educational leadership. Educational Administration Quarterly 27, no. 2: 185–201.

———. 1994. Building an ethical school: A practical response to the moral crisis in schools. London: Falmer Press.

ADDITIONAL RESOURCES

Mullen, C. A., and K. C. Robertson. 2014. Shifting to lead: The politics of black and white identity in school leadership. Charlotte, NC: Information Age.

Palmer, P. 1998. The courage to teach. San Francisco: Jossey-Bass.

Pellicer, L. 1999. Caring enough to lead: Schools and the sacred trust. Thousand Oaks, CA: Corwin Press.

Rebore, R. W. 2013. The ethics of leadership. 2nd ed. Boston: Pearson.

Ruggiero, V. R. 1988. The art of thinking. 2nd ed. New York: Harper Collins.

Snowden, P., and R. Gorton. 1998. School leadership and administration: Important concepts, case studies, and simulations. 5th ed. New York: McGraw-Hill.

Chapter Four

Bridging the Digital Divide

Texas Principal Exam Competency 004: The principal knows how to facilitate the design and implementation of curricula and strategic plans that enhance teaching and learning; ensure alignment of curriculum, instruction, resources, and assessment; and measure student performance.

Texas Chapter 149 Standard 1 (2014): The principal is responsible for ensuring every student receives high-quality instruction.

ELCC Standard 2.0: (2011): A building-level education leader applies knowledge that promotes the success of every student by sustaining a school culture and instructional program conducive to student learning through collaboration, trust, and a personalized learning environment with high expectations for students; creating and evaluating a comprehensive, rigorous, and coherent curricular and instructional school program; developing and supervising the instructional and leadership capacity of school staff; and promoting the most effective and appropriate technologies to support teaching and learning within a school environment.

ABSTRACT

The cases in this chapter focus on the integration of technology in the instructional program, specifically the challenges of using new technology. In the first case, the principal needs to provide professional development in the use of iPads and interactive whiteboard, and in the second case, the principal must review the iPad usage policy with the students, teachers, and parents.

51

Specific procedures for misuse of the policy should be developed and shared with all stakeholders.

OBJECTIVES

1. The principal knows how to facilitate effective campus curriculum planning based on knowledge of emerging issues, principles of curriculum design, and student learning data.
2. The principal demonstrates the ability to analyze curriculum to ensure that teachers align content across all disciplines.
3. The principal demonstrates the ability to assist school personnel in recognizing, celebrating, and incorporating diversity in programs, curriculum, and instructional practices.
4. The principal understands how to use the most effective and appropriate technologies to support teaching and learning in a school environment.
5. The principal demonstrates the ability to sustain a school culture and instructional program conducive to student learning.

LITERATURE REVIEW

As cries for school reform resonate throughout the nation, school districts in the twenty-first century are vigorously involved with educational reform strategies. One major reform is the integration of technology into the schools. Curriculum and instruction revisions are major components of this reform effort. Teachers need the support and direction of the building principal and school district leadership in order to make the appropriate changes in their teaching, pedagogy, and technology integration. Thus, the role of principal as instructional leader is vitally important to the success of technology integration. The instructional leaders must be aware of the sophisticated information and communication technologies that are changing the nature of instructional delivery.

In order to encourage the integration of technology in schools, the International Society for Technology in Education (ISTE) developed national standards. These standards are the following: (a) visionary leadership, (b) digital age learning culture, (c) excellence in professional practice, (d) systemic improvement, and (e) digital leadership. These standards are the skills and knowledge that school administrators and leaders need to successfully integrate technology in their schools (ISTE 2009).

However, Peck, Mullen, Lashley, and Eldridge's (2011) study found major challenges when integrating technology into the schools such as: "(a) weak support structures that affected the implementation and maintenance of technology, (b) teachers' conflicting roles of encouraging technology use while also discouraging the students use of personal media devices (i.e., cell phones and MP3 players), and (c) students with more technology knowledge than teachers that were able to find ways around school rules" (43).

Principal as Instructional Leader

The role of instructional leadership emerged in the early 1980s, which called for a paradigm shift from management to leadership. This shift was influenced by the effective schools research (Brookover and Lezotte 1982). Recently however, instructional leadership has made a comeback. This new focus on instructional leadership was caused by the increasing importance placed on the needs for schools to be held accountable for all students' success (Jenkins 2009). Instructional leadership includes a deeper involvement in the teaching and learning process (DuFour 2002).

As an instructional leader, the principal plays a crucial role in the school by influencing the quality of teacher instruction and student achievement. Robinson, Lloyd, and Rowe (2008) found that the average effect of instructional leadership on student outcomes was three to four times that of transformational leadership. Therefore, the more principals focus their professional relationships, their work, and their learning on the core business of teaching and learning, the greater their influence on student outcomes have been.

Certainly, instruction is not the sole responsibility of the principal, but the principal is responsible for providing instructional support to ensure that quality instruction is provided for all students. Seashore-Louis, Leithwood, Wahlstrom, and Anderson (2010) suggested that principals provide instructional support by emphasizing the value of research-based strategies and applying them effectively to their own school; by encouraging teacher collaboration, providing more time for teacher planning, and by monitoring their teachers' work (Wallace Foundation 2012).

While principal autonomy is important, principals as instructional leaders need the support of the district and school board members to bring about school improvement. Bottoms and Schmidt-Davis (2010, 7) identified several ways districts can provide this support:

- Develop tools and processes principals can use to ensure instruction is aligned to the district's goals and standards;
- Invest in high-quality professional development for principals and teachers;
- Set a culture and a structure for the use of data to guide instructional improvement.

Implementation of Technology in Schools

Appropriate technology use in schools can not only be beneficial in increasing students' learning outcome and motivation, but also improve teacher's satisfaction and school principals' effectiveness (Weng and Tang 2014). However, technology in and of itself may not have the inherent power to change teaching and learning practices (Blackwell, Lauricella, and Wartella 2014).

Thus, ongoing professional development for school leaders is essential for successful technology initiatives. Leading a technology-transformed school calls for different skills from those needed in a traditional industrial-age school. In order to meaningfully integrate technology into curriculum and instruction, leaders must transform traditional beliefs and teachers must rework traditional teaching practices so that robustly infused technology can create a generative teaching and learning environment (Klimek, Ritzenhein, and Sullivan 2008).

Mobile Technology

Kiger, Herro, and Prunty (2012) found that mobile technology improves student engagement, peer interaction, and collaboration, and is used to collect feedback and improve communication, extending classroom learning as well as being cost effective for students in kindergarten through twelfth-grade classrooms. Negdungadi and Raman (2012) stated that mobile devices are now affordable and widespread, with most school students having a parent with a mobile phone or one of their own. The availability of mobile phones and tablets with Web access make these devices accessible for learning (Negdungadi and Raman 2012).

The mobile technologies have impacted schools. Many schools have created ubiquitous learning using mobile devices for each student (Project RED 2010). These schools understand that ubiquitous learning is not bound by the school day or by classroom walls:

> Ubiquitous computing includes the idea that both teachers and students are active participants in the learning process, who critically analyze information, create new knowledge in a variety of ways (both collaboratively and individually), communicate what they have learned, and choose which tools are appropriate for a particular task. (Brodzik 2012, 5)

The one-to-one laptop or mobile learning programs enable schools to prepare students for the "rapidly changing future and knowledge of twenty-first-century skills" (Gallagher 2011, 2).

Barriers

Ertmer, Addison, Lane, Ross, and Woods (1999) posited that certain first-order and second-order barriers exist that may prevent teachers from successfully integrating technology into their classroom. The first-order barriers were: "(a) lack of access to technology, (b) time to learn and use technology, (c) training and support, and (d) professional development. Second-order barriers were: (a) teacher attitude and beliefs about the value of technology, and (b) teacher comfort with technology" (1). Today, teachers have more access to technology and professional development (Gray, Thomas, and Lewis 2010); however, their attitudes, confidence and anxiety about use of technology correlate with actual use (Ertmer, Ottenbreit-Leftwich, Sadik, Sendurur, and Sendurur 2012; Lindahl and Folkesson 2012).

Role of the Instructional Leader

Teachers cannot be expected to successfully integrate technology in their classrooms without the support of the leadership in their school. This support may include (a) enabling teachers to use technology, (b) building leadership in others; and (c) developing a clear vision regarding ways in which technology can support learning" (Langran 2006, iv). In addition, principals as instructional leaders can facilitate the successful integration of technology in schools by:

- Engaging the whole school in a discussion about how they as a community want to adopt mobile technology and what it can mean.
- Adequate investment in professional development and support for staff (not in how to use the technology, but how to think about integrating technology into their practice).

- The inclusive development of policies and frameworks (where students' ideas are considered and respected, not tokenistic) that do not limit the value of having the technology in the first place.
- Trusting and supporting students and teachers to become thoughtful and purposeful digital citizens who are part of an ongoing process of improving our learning culture. (Donahoo 2012, 20)

Reforming Education through Strategic Design

Peters and Waterman (1983) studied organizations that had successfully made fundamental changes and identified a new paradigm of organizational functioning that focused on the future, personal empowerment, purpose-driven action, and flexibility. In other words, they stressed better utilization of all stakeholders and challenged leaders to reform around realities about learners and life. Spady (2002) furthered this line of thought regarding reforming education into a strategic design process called the "total learning community." In order for an education system's direction to be strategic, it must have the following characteristics:

- Be learner centered, which means asking about the capacities, interests, and motivations of students;
- Be future focused, which means asking about the conditions students face when their formal education is complete;
- Be research based, which means asking about the best knowledge available about learners and their future in order to design and implement empowering learning experiences.

Thus, planning curriculum with a strategic design strategy causes the curriculum to be a vehicle for student learning rather than a goal in itself. This challenges principals to consider a more visionary approach that focuses on empowerment and embraces all learners where "education is not the goal; life beyond education is" (Spady 2002, 60).

Additionally, DuFour (2002) commented that for years as a principal, he saw his role as instructional leader as observing teachers and asking, "What are the teachers teaching?" and "How can I help them to teach it more effectively?" Eventually, as a veteran principal, he realized that he should have been asking, "To what extent are the students learning the intended outcomes of each course?" and "What steps can I take to give both students and teachers the additional time and support they need to improve learning?"

(13). In other words, principals who are instructional leaders, even more, are "learning leaders." As learning leaders, they examine school efforts through the lens of learning, which has a substantive effect on the culture of the school as it moves from helping individual teachers to helping teams of teachers focus on student achievement.

Relatedly, when Bushman, Goodman, Brown-Welty, and Dorn (2001), in a California study, asked school principals about what school reform efforts were being implemented in their schools to improve the education of the lowest-achieving students, their responses overwhelmingly indicated that principals were emphasizing being instructional leaders. They identified several ways that they were focusing more on individualizing instruction by looking at the data, identifying available programs, and expanding the schedule to involve new configurations. Additionally, these principals focused on curriculum articulation and alignment, improved student-centered methodologies, and greater involvement of parents.

CASE STUDY

In October 2014 voters in Adkins school district approved an $87.68 million bond package. One of the bond projects passed was for district-wide instructional technology improvements. Every teacher in the school district received an iPad as well as an interactive whiteboard. Teachers were stressed about how to integrate both the iPad and the interactive whiteboard into their classroom instruction. Teachers experienced difficulties with the iPads because the district's wireless capabilities could not handle the high volume of wireless traffic. Teachers were overwhelmed by learning to teach using the technology. In addition, as principal, you have noticed an increase in office referrals from the same teachers who were most stressed over the technology.

DISCUSSION

Create a PowerPoint presentation to present to the superintendent and faculty that outlines what can you do as a principal to facilitate the implementation of these technology devices.

1. What can you do as an administrator to help teachers with technology integration?

2. What can you do to support the teachers so their frustrations do not result in classroom management problems?
3. How can you advocate and support teachers in their attempts to use the technology?
4. Identify schools in your area that have implemented mobile devices. Interview the principals about professional development provided to teachers on the integration of the mobile devices in classroom instruction.
5. Using the same schools in question four, interview some of the teachers about their perception of how the principals provide support, resources, and professional development for the integration of mobile devices in classroom instruction.
6. Interview principals of several different schools regarding their understanding of the principal's role as instructional leader as related to the use of technology.

ON YOUR OWN—CONSIDER

Happy ISD began a new Gifted and Talented program in the fall of 2013 for students in first through sixth grade. Students were required to pass an achievement test to be eligible for the program. During the first year of implementation there were forty-four students and each student received an iPad. This is the first time that Happy ISD purchased an electronic device for students to use at school and home. All parents were expected to sign a technology usage form to use any type of technology device such as computers or iPads. Students were given an iPad to use for activities while at school and were able to take them home.

To help ensure iPads were not broken due to incidental drops, the school district purchased protective rubber cases. Prior to students receiving the iPads parents signed a waiver stating that they understood students should keep their iPads in the protective cases as well as use the iPad for educational purposes.

The vast majority of the students abided by the rules and used the iPad for educational reasons only. However, one student began searching inappropriate subjects online. Teachers and parents were made aware of these searches so the student was given a warning. The inappropriate search stopped briefly but then started again when the student thought people had forgotten. Since the student was not able to make good decisions about the searches, the iPad was taken away. However, since the iPad was used frequently during the Gifted and Talented class, the student was issued the iPad only during the Gifted and Talented class. After a month, the student was allowed to take the iPad home again with clear expectations given to her parents that the iPad was to be used for educational purposes only. The student and parents agreed that they understood the guidelines and would follow the rules.

Another problem surfaced: The student began taking the iPad out of the case although she knew this was against the rules. Despite several warnings by the teacher, the student continued to take the iPad out of the protective case and dropped it. The iPad hit the floor and the screen cracked in several places.

You are the principal. What will you do?

REMEMBER

The principal demonstrates the ability to sustain a school culture and instructional program conducive to student learning through collaboration, trust, and personalized learning environment with high expectations of all students.

REFERENCES

Blackwell, C. K., A. R. Lauricella, and E. Wartella. 2014. Factors influencing digital technology use in early childhood education. Retrieved from dx.doi.org/10.10.1016/j.compedu.2014. 040130360-1315 @ Elsevier Ltd.

Bottoms, G., and J. Schmidt-Davis. 2010. The Three Essentials: Improving schools requires district vision, district and state support, and principal leadership. Southern Regional Education Board. Retrieved from www.wallacefoundation.org/knowledge-center/school-leader ship/district-policy-and-practice/Documents/Three-Essentials-to-Improving-Schools.pdf.

Brodzik, M. C. 2012. An implementation plan: One-to-one laptop program recommendations for the Pittsgrove Township School District. EdD, Wilmington University, Delaware. ProQuest Dissertations and Theses (926432739).

Brookover, W. B., and L. Lezotte. 1982. Creating effective schools. Holmes Beach, FL: Learning Publication.

Bushman, J., G. Goodman, S. Brown-Welty, and S. Dorn. 2001. California testing: How principals chose priorities. Educational Leadership 59, no. 1: 33–37.

Donahoo, D. 2012. The challenges of 1:1 in the classroom. Retrieved from www.nmc.org/ news/challenges-11-classroom.

DuFour, R. 2002. The learning-centered principal. Educational Leadership 59, no. 8: 12–15.

Ertmer, P. A., P. M. Addison, M. Lane, E. Ross, and D. Woods. 1999. Examining teachers' beliefs about the role of technology in the elementary classroom. Journal of Research on Computing in Education 32: 1, 2, 54–72.

Ertmer, P. A., A. T. Ottenbreit-Leftwich, O. Sadik, E. Sendurer, and P. Sendurur. 2012. Teachers' belief and technology integration practices: A critical relationship. Computers & Education 59: 2, 423–35, dx.doi.org/10/1016/j. compedu.2010.02.001.

Gallagher, F. 2011. The partnership for 21st century learning. Retrieved from www.p21.org/.

Gray, L., M. Thomas, and L. Lewis. 2010. Teachers' use of educational technology in US public schools: 2009 (NCES 2010-040). Washington, DC: National Center for Education Statistics, Institute for Education Sciences, U.S. Department of Education. Retrieved from nces.ed.gov/pubs2010/2010040.pdf.

Hoy, A., and W. Hoy. 2003. Instructional leadership: A learning-centered guide. Boston: Allyn & Bacon.

International Society for Technology in Education (ISTE). 2009. National Education Technology Standards for Administrators. Retrieved from www.iste.org/ docs/pdfs/nets-a-standards. pdf.

Jenkins, B. 2009. What it takes to be an instructional leader. Principal 88, no. 3: 34–37.

Kiger, D., D. Herro, and D. Prunty. 2012. Examining the influence of a mobile learning intervention on third grade math achievement. Journal of Research on Technology in Education 45: 1, 61.

Klimek, K. J, E. Ritzenhein, and K. D. Sullivan. 2008. Generative leadership: Shaping new futures for today's schools. Thousand Oaks, CA: Corwin Press.

Langran, E. 2006. Technology leadership: How principals, technology coordinators, and technology interact in K–12 schools. PhD, University of Virginia. ProQuest Dissertations and Theses (304961826).

Leithwood, K., K. S. Louis, S. Anderson, and K. Wahlstrom. 2004. How leadership influences student learning. Wallace Foundation. Retrieved from www.wallacefoundation.org/ knowledge-center/school-leadership/key-research/Pages/How-Leadership-Influences-Student-Learning.aspx.

Lindahl, M., and A. Folkesson. 2012. ICT in preschool: Friend or foe? The significance of norms in a changing practice. International Journal of Early Years Education 20: 422–36.

Monson, M., and R. Monson. 1993. Who creates the curriculum: New roles for teachers. Educational Leadership 2: 19–21.

Negdungadi, P., and R. Raman. 2012. A new approach to personalization: Integrating e-learning and m-learning. Education Tech Research Dev 60: 659.

Peck, C., C. A. Mullen, C. Lashley, and J. A. Eldridge. 2011. School leadership and technology challenges: Lessons from a new American high school. AASA Journal of Scholarship and Practice 7: 39–51.

Robinson, V. M. J., C. A. Lloyd, and K. J. Rowe. 2008. The impact of leadership on student outcomes: An analysis of the differential effects of leadership types. Educational Administration Quarterly 44, no. 5: 63.

Seashore-L., K. Leithwood, K. L. Wahlstrom, and S. E. Anderson. 2010. Learning from leadership: Investigating the links to improved student learning. Center for Applied Research and Education Improvement, University of Missouri, Ontario Institute at the University of Toronto: Wallace Foundation.

Spady, W. 2002. Re-forming the reforms: How total leaders face education's biggest challenge. Principal Leadership 2, no. 5: 57–62.

Wallace Foundation. 2012. The school principal as leader: Guiding schools to better teaching and learning. Wallace Foundation. Retrieved from www.wallacefoundation.org/knowledge-center/school-leadership/effective-principal-leadership/Documents/The-School-Principal-as-Leader-Guiding-Schools-to-Better-Teaching-and-Learning.pdf.

Wang, M. C., G. D. Haertel, and H. J. Walberg. 1993. Toward a knowledge base for school learning. Review of Educational Research 63: 249–94.

———. 1997. Learning influences. In Psychology and educational practice (199–211). Edited by H. Walberg and G. Haertel. Berkeley, CA: McCutchan.

Weng, C.-H., and Y. Tang. 2014. The relationship between technology leadership strategies and effectiveness of school administration: An empirical study. Retrieved from dx.doi.org/1016/j.compedu.2014.030100360-1315@ Elsevier Ltd.

ADDITIONAL RESOURCES

Anderson, R. E., and S. Dexter. 2005. School technology leadership: An empirical investigation of prevalence and effect. Educational Administration Quarterly 40, no. 1: 49–82.

Beglau, M. 2011. Supervising teachers' technology use. Principal Leadership, 64–66. Retrieved from www.setda.org/c/document_library/get_file? folderId=300&name=DLFE-1233.pdf.

Conn, C. 2011. Using technology for assessing and evaluating student learning and instructional practices. In Technology leadership for school improvement (231–51). Edited by R. Papa. Thousand Oaks, CA: Sage.

Creighton, T. 2003. The principal as technology leader. Thousand Oaks, CA: Corwin Press.

———. 2011. Entrepreneurial leadership for technology: An opposable mind. In Technology leadership for school improvement (3–20). Thousand Oaks, CA: Sage.

Daniel, T. K., and J. Nance. 2002. The role of the administrator in instructional technology policy. Brigham Young University Education & Law Journal, 1–2.

Davies, P. 2010. On school educational technology leadership. Management in Education 24, no. 2: 55–61. doi:10.1177/0892020610363089.

Dawson, C., and G. Rakes. 2003. The influence of principals' technology training on the integration of technology in schools. Journal of Research on Technology in Education 36, no.1: 29–49. Retrieved from cmapspublic2.ihmc.us/rid=1133304866250_585937957_2778/dawson.pdf.

Glatthorn, A. A. 2001. The principal as curriculum leader. 2nd ed. Thousand Oaks, CA: Corwin Press.

Papa, R. 2011. Technology leadership for school improvement. Thousand Oaks, CA: Sage.

Prensky, M. 2010. Teaching digital natives, partnering for real learning. Thousand Oaks, CA: Corwin Press.

Chapter Five

The Best Surprise Is No Surprise

Texas Principal Exam Competency 005: The principal knows how to advocate, nurture, and sustain an instructional program and a campus culture that are conducive to student learning and staff professional growth.

Texas Chapter 149 Standard 1 (2014): The principal is responsible for ensuring every student receives high-quality instruction.

Texas Chapter 149 Standard III (2014): The principal is responsible for modeling a consistent focus on and commitment to improving student learning.

Texas Chapter 149 Standard IV (2014): The principal is responsible for establishing and implementing a shared vision and culture of high expectations for all staff and students.

ELCC Standard 1.0 (2011): A building-level education leader applies knowledge that promotes the success of every student by collaboratively facilitating the development, articulation, implementation, and stewardship of a shared school vision of learning. This process is done through the collection and use of data to identify school goals, assess organizational effectiveness, and implement school plans to achieve school goals.

ELCC Standard 2.0 (2011): A building-level education leader applies knowledge that promotes the success of every student by sustaining a school culture and instructional program conducive to student learning through collaboration, trust, and personalized learning environment.

ELCC Standard 6.0 (2011): A building-level education leader applies knowledge that promotes the success of every student by understanding, responding to, and influencing the larger political, social, economic, legal, and cultural context.

ABSTRACT

Both cases in this chapter focus on the instructional program, the difficulty of bringing change to a campus, and the need for faculty professional development that focuses on student needs. In one case, the principal needs to motivate a faculty to implement changes in the instructional program for the entire campus, and in the second case, the principal must focus on one teacher whose teaching practices reflect a lack of sensitivity to all the students in her class.

OBJECTIVES

1. The principal has the ability to facilitate activities that apply principles of effective instruction to improve instructional practices and curricular materials.
2. The principal has the ability to assist school personnel in understanding and applying best practices for student learning.
3. The principal has the ability to use strategies such as observations, collaborative reflection, and adult learning strategies to form comprehensive professional growth plans with faculty.
4. The principal assesses school culture using multiple methods and implements strategies that capitalize on the diversity of the school community to improve school programs and culture.
5. The principal can understand, collect, and use data to identify school goals, assess organizational effectiveness, and implement plans to achieve school goals.
6. The principal can understand, create, and evaluate a comprehensive, rigorous, and coherent curricular and instructional program.
7. The principal can understand and act to influence local, district, state, and national decisions affecting student learning in a school environment.

LITERATURE REVIEW

Today, concerns about the quality of education provided to our children and the demands that school reform must occur are at an all-time high. However, often attempts to bring about school reform, though well-intended, fail to accomplish the needed goal.

Fullan and Miles (1992) argued that this happens because educators rarely address the substantive need for the amount of work involved to bring about reform. Hargreaves (1994) attributed failure to mandating new teaching methods that fail to consider practicality, while Schmoker (1996) argued that the "initiatives du jour" fail because they do not address student learning (2). Despite past decades of school reform to advance all students' achievement little progress is evident.

Research suggests that successful school reforms occur when multiple elements are in place, including strong school leadership, increased teachers' professional capacity for instruction, student-centered instruction, and links to parents and the community. These features cannot occur without supportive, shared school culture norms (Kaplan and Owings 2013). Certainly, most would agree with Fullan's (1997) assessment that there is no one "silver bullet" (41) that brings about educational reform; instead, reform issues must be integrated with other efforts that focus on improving schools.

Change Strategies for Reform

Combs, Edmonson, and Harris (2013) argue that a major factor in creating an environment for change is building a climate of trust where it is safe to take risks and express differing points of view. When this occurs, conflict often emerges. Therefore, principals are challenged to view conflict as a positive change effort and provide an avenue for discourse where conflicting ideas are welcomed as sources of information and insight.

Combs and colleagues (2013) suggest that to incorporate trust-building strategies, leaders must first acknowledge actions that are considered "trust busters." Trust busters include such actions as not listening to input, ignoring incompetence, reprimanding the group rather than individuals, and gossiping. Trust builders consist of actions that build trust and actions that boost and sustain trust. Trust builders include such strategies as listening actively, building consensus, being consistent, being empathetic, maintaining confidentiality using power wisely, and empowering others. Trust boosters emphasize ongoing assessment of trust levels, talking about trust, recognizing talent, allowing people to fail, and providing resources.

Organizations go through three overlapping phases as change occurs: mobilization, implementation, and institutionalization (Berman and McLaughlin 1978). Mobilization incorporates initial planning efforts that include the development of a team of interested stakeholders and identifies needed resources to support the change. Implementation involves professional development with follow-up training and feedback. This phase also encourages needed modifications. The final phase, institutionalization, is marked by acceptance or rejection of the change.

Of course, change also occurs on the personal level. A recommended change strategy for avoiding conflict at this level is the Concerns-Based Adoption Model (CBAM), which emphasizes the individuals involved and the innovation as a primary concern (Hord, Rutherford, Huling-Austin, and Gall 1987). The stages of concern include the following:

- Awareness—providing information
- Information—finding out more about the suggested change
- Personal—asking how it will affect me
- Management—inviting users to demonstrate how they managed the innovation
- Consequence—wondering how it will affect students
- Collaboration—relating ways that instructors can work together to integrate change
- Refocusing—discussing how the innovation can be enhanced or improved

Another strategy for reducing conflict during the change process is to create a school leadership team. The school leadership team may comprise influential faculty, assistant principals, special programs representatives, and parents and community members who can provide a supportive environment during the change implementation. The leadership team determines where the organization needs to go by: (a) assessing the school's goals and data to identify areas of improvement; (b) set clear, measurable goals for school improvement; (c) create small wins; (d) build partnerships with parent and community members; and (e) sustain communication and collaboration (Kaplan and Owings 2013).

Harris (2000) suggested that in order to create a climate within our schools that fosters successful change efforts, principals must consider five critical factors that revolve around asking a central question: What is best for students? These factors include (a) creating a culture that is supportive and inviting for students, faculty, and the learning community; (b) establishing collaborative leadership that is communicated into every area of the school; (c) clarifying accountability strategies to reflect student-centered progress; (d) encouraging teachers to be committed to a care ethic; and (e) implementing change strategies that "strike at the heart of how children learn and how teachers teach" (Hargreaves 1994, 11).

Professional Learning Communities

Leadership comes in many forms and is most effective when shared to create collective responsibility for change. Hord (1997), an internationally known pioneer in the field of school improvement, defined Professional Learning Communities (PLCs) as the professional staff learning together to direct efforts toward improved student learning. Thus, PLCs allow teachers and principals to become shared leaders and develop capacity within all members to share authority without one person dominating (Hord 1997).

Four purposes of PLCs exist, which include: (a) promote student learning, (b) promote adult learning, (c) professionalize teacher practice, and (d) change education. Since change in education is a common purpose of PLCs, leaders play a key role in initiating and sustaining change through monitoring the progress of PLCs and actively promoting changes in instruction, curriculum and assessment (Foord and Haar 2008).

There are five principles of change that have implications for the implementation of effective PLCs. These principles are: "(a) change in practices lead to changes in beliefs, (b) change comes when teachers share a common concern and commit to changes because of a common purpose, (d) change in practice requires clear target for effective professional practices and frequent feedback on performance, (d) change in practices includes understanding, personalizing, operationalizing and evaluating the practices, and (e) effective change can be enhanced by monitoring the level of use of new practices" (Foord and Haar 2008, 10–11)

Effective PLCs must be sustained. Leaders sustain PLCs through continuous monitoring and assessing progress of implementation. Hall and Hord's (2001) level of use protocol can be used to sustain PLCs through assessing progress of implementation. Foord and Haar (2008) modified Hall and Hord's (2001) level of use protocol to categorize data about change implementation. Foord and Hall's protocol consists of levels of change and includes a description of each level:

- *Level 0.* **No use**—user has no knowledge or involvement in change.
- *Level 1.* **Orientation**—recently acquired or is acquiring information about innovation or change.
- *Level 2.* **Preparation**—preparing for first use of innovation or change.
- *Level 3.* **Mechanical**—short-term, day-to-day innovation and/or change with little reflection, superficial use, or change.
- *Level 4A.* **Routine**—Use and change are stabilized. Few, if any, ongoing changes are being made.
- *Level 4B.* **Refinement**—User varies the use and/or change to increase impact on students. Variation is based on knowledge of consequences for students.
- *Level 5.* **Integration**—User combines own efforts to change, with related activities of colleagues to achieve a collective impact on students.
- *Level 6.* **Renewal**—User reevaluates the quality of changes, seeks major modifications or alternatives to increase impact on students, examines new developments in the field, and explores new goals for self and system.

Leaders can ask the following questions to determine the level of implementation of PLCs:

- Are there changes in beliefs and practices about effective teaching and learning?
- Are there plans to change in the future?
- Are you seeking more information about the change?
- What kind of changes are happening in beliefs or practices?
- What led to these changes?
- Are you planning modification or changes? (Foord and Haar 2008)

Educate Every Child to High Levels

A critical role of the principal and teachers in professional learning communities is to recognize the importance of addressing cultural, racial, and ethnic diversity in the school. The United States is currently undergoing one of the most pivotal demographic transformations in history. In fact, the U.S. Census Bureau (2012) predicted that Latinos, African Americans, Asian Americans,

Native Americans, and Pacific Islanders will collectively become the majority population in the United States by 2042. By 2050 students of color are expected to account for 54 percent of the U.S. population. Non-Latino whites will represent the remaining 46 percent, down from their current 63.7 percent share (U.S. Census Bureau 2012).

There are several research-based best practices that can be implemented in classrooms to ensure that we successfully educate all children. One best practice is to create a student-centered learning culture within the school. A student-centered learning culture consists of: (a) developing high teacher expectations for all students; (b) creating a safe, caring, and intellectually challenging environment; (c) teaching all children for intellectual excellence and rigor; and (d) providing academic support by using instructional and assessment techniques that intentionally account for individual uniqueness (Kaplan and Owings 2013).

Another research-based best practice is the use of culturally responsive teaching in the classroom. Culturally responsive teaching involves educators' use of diverse students' cultural knowledge, prior experiences, and learning styles to make learning more appropriate and effective (Gay 2000). Culturally diverse teachers provide inclusive educational programming that respects cultural differences and relates learning to students' cultures.

Villegas and Lucas (2002) argued that when teachers exhibit an affirming attitude toward students with diverse backgrounds, they greatly affect their learning, belief in self, and overall academic achievement. Culturally responsive teachers provide connections between students' prior knowledge and what they need to know. They learn about their students' past experiences as well as their home and community cultures in order to establish relationships and incorporate students' experiences in teaching and learning contexts. These educators use a constructivist approach to facilitate all students' critical thinking, problem solving, collaboration, and multiple perspectives. Ladson-Billings (1992) posited that culturally responsive teachers use "cultural referents to impart knowledge, skills, and attitudes" (382) to help students develop to their fullest potentials.

Professional learning communities should employ the tools of cultural proficiency to guide the teaching and learning process. These tools include: (a) acknowledging culture as a predominant force in shaping behaviors, values, and institutions; (b) understanding that people are served in varying degrees by the dominant culture; (c) recognizing that the group identity of individuals is as important as their individual identities; (d) knowing that diversity within cultures is vast and significant; (e) understanding that each group has unique cultural needs; and (f) recognizing that the best of both worlds enhances the capacity of all (CampbellJones, CampbellJones, and Lindsey 2009).

While there may be barriers to cultural proficiency such as resistance to change, systems of oppression, and a sense of privilege and entitlement, professional learning communities can overcome these barriers by integrating the essential elements of cultural competence within the teaching and learning environment, which include: (a) assessing cultural knowledge; (b) valuing diversity; (c) managing the dynamics of difference; (d) adapting to diversity; and (e) institutionalizing cultural knowledge (CampbellJones, CampbellJones, and Lindsey 2009).

CASE STUDY 1

Shady Grove Elementary School had been slow to change. The building looked just like it did the year it was built—1967. Many of the teaching practices mirrored the authoritarian instructional models that were no longer considered effective. The organizational structure of thirty self-contained classrooms, kindergarten through fourth grade, did not include communication between teachers on curriculum, instructional strategies, or assessment. Teachers taught their classes, implemented the district's curriculum, and were considered successful if they sent few discipline situations to the office.

After longtime principal Serena Foster had retired last year, new principal Brian Williams was anxious to make changes. A recent graduate of the Midstate University Educational Leadership Program, Brian was determined to lead Shady Grove Elementary School in becoming a student-centered school. He knew and understood the importance of capitalizing on diversity and making decisions based on sound research and best practice and using school and district data. He had a strong knowledge base and excellent communication skills. But he was met with a huge surprise. The Shady Grove Elementary School teachers did not want changes in their school.

Brian learned quickly that the practice of assigning students to classes was in fact a tracking system with low-, middle-, and high-performing classes in each grade. Incoming kindergarten students were assigned to groups using kindergarten-readiness tests, and those student groups were then maintained in first and second grades as well. Third- and fourth-grade students were assigned to homogeneous groups based on the previous year's state assessment scores. Brian was dismayed to learn that few students moved higher than their original classification. Students who were assigned to the low or middle groups in kindergarten tended to stay in the low and/or middle groups the rest of their time at Shady Grove Elementary School.

Brian also learned quickly that some teachers had never taught the lower-performing groups of children. Veteran fourth-grade teacher Vera Spencer told him that she had always taught the "high" group. "I don't teach those low kids; my expertise is with the high-performing students. I understand their needs, and I really challenge them. When they leave my room, they're ready for fifth grade."

Conversely, third-grade teacher Betty Sue Hamilton always taught a "low" group of students. She described her teaching philosophy to Brian: "Well, you know, we must make allowances for these students. Many of them come from really terrible home situations, and I tailor my instruction to their levels. I always take them where they are, and they always have such a good school year with me. We don't expect them to do the same work that the higher groups do."

Students were already assigned to classes when Brian assumed the principalship last July. Now in his first year as principal, he is determined that the tracking system will be changed.

CASE STUDY 2

Martha Strong, senior English teacher at Clear Springs High School, had sponsored a trip to England during spring break for her senior students each year for the past fourteen years. There had been some concerns that the trip, while it was certainly not a requirement for senior English, had some bearing on grades. It had been reported through the years that Martha discussed the trip at length during class, planned activities for those students who would be making the trip, and then conducted in-depth discussions of the sites visited in the weeks after the trip. Students who did not participate had reported that they felt left out of class discussions and that the annual trip promoted an elitist group of students.

On several occasions, Clear Springs High School principal Wanda Bruce had talked with Martha about the trip. Martha always explained that the trip was not a class requirement, that parents accompanied the students serving as chaperones, that she had never had any problem with students, and that it was an excellent educational opportunity for seniors. While she acknowledged that the trip was expensive and that not every student could afford it, she also pointed out, "Just because some kids can't go, should we deny the opportunity for those who can afford it? Just as every student can't attend a private university, we don't close them because everyone can't afford to go there."

Now, not surprisingly, Wanda was in her office, waiting for still another conference with Martha and three parents of senior students who had not gone to England this past month. Their children reported that they were disenfranchised in Martha's class because they had not gone, that several students made fun of them, and that Martha had allowed students who went on the trip to submit an essay on their activities for an extra-credit assignment. Wanda listened as the parents described their concerns and arranged a conference that would begin in ten minutes. She thought, "Why am I not surprised? Here we go again, same song, fourteenth verse."

DISCUSSION QUESTIONS

1. If you were principal of the school in case 1, what is the first thing that you would do to bring about change to this campus? Support your answer.
2. Design a long-term campus plan for the principal to implement that would bring about needed educational reform to this campus.
3. Would you use the same change strategies in case 2 that you used in case 1? Identify how you would solve the issue in case 2.
4. How might your strategies differ or be like the strategies used to solve case 1?
5. Discuss the ethical implications of each of these case studies.
6. What types of assessment data could be gathered to help improve the decision process in both case 1 and case 2?
7. Structure a professional learning community for the school in case 1.
8. Interview a first-year principal or reflect on your first year as principal. What types of changes were needed on campus, and how did you identify these?
9. Identify a major reform issue to be implemented on your campus (or use tracking in case 1), gather five research articles, and write a three- to five-page report that will be shared with the class.
10. With a partner or in small groups, construct a plan for a culturally diverse school to ensure that all students are provided a high-quality, flexible instructional program. Identify services that your plan will

provide for at-risk students and resources that will be needed to implement the program.

ON YOUR OWN—CONSIDER

South Pacific Elementary School is one of the elementary schools in the Richland Hills School District. It has undergone major changes in the past six years. The student population has more than doubled with no signs of stopping. Not only did the school need more buildings, materials, and additional staff to accommodate the overwhelming growth, but they found they did not have the knowledge and skills to respond to the newly found diversity among the staff and the students.

Because of the staggering new student population growth, a variety of cultures have emerged that were different from that of the staff and students previously enrolled in the school. The members of the Professional Learning Communities (PLCs) identified a goal of change to embrace the unique culture of all the students and to create a safe, caring learning environment for everyone at South Pacific Elementary School. Working with their Parent Teachers Association, they adopted the slogan "We are Family." They envisioned all members—students, parents, educators, and community—as family.

From the start, the PLCs embarked on a journey toward cultural proficiency to help them respond to the growing population of new staff and students. Most of the staff agreed and thought the approach would enhance their knowledge and skills and strengthen relationships. Only a few thought the journey was a waste of time. "We are all Americans. I don't know why this cultural proficiency stuff is necessary in the first place," was a typical response from the dissenters.

REMEMBER

The principal assesses school culture using multiple methods and implements strategies that capitalize on the diversity of the school community to improve school programs and culture.

REFERENCES

Bagin, D., and D. Gallagher. 2001. The school and community relations. 7th ed. Boston: Allyn & Bacon.

Banks, J. 1999. An introduction to multicultural education. 2nd ed. Boston: Allyn & Bacon.

Burnett, G. 1995. Alternatives to ability grouping: Still unanswered questions. Report No. EDO-UD-95-8. ERIC Document Reproduction Service No. ED 390 947 (111). New York: ERIC Clearinghouse on Urban Education.

CampbellJones, F., B. CampbellJones, and R. B. Lindsey. 2010. The cultural proficiency journey: Moving beyond ethical barriers toward profound school change. Thousand Oaks, CA: Corwin Press.

Combs, J., S. Edmonson, and S. Harris. 2013. The trust factor. New York: Routledge.

Fullan, M., and M. Miles. 1992. Getting reform right: What works and what doesn't? Phi Delta Kappan 73, no. 10: 745–52.

Gay, G. 2000. Culturally responsive teaching. New York: Teachers College Press.

Hall, G. E., and S. M. Hord. 2001. Implementing change: Patterns, principles, and potholes. Boston: Allyn & Bacon.

Hargreaves, A. 1994. Changing teachers, changing times. New York: Teachers College Press.

Harris, S. 2000. Creating a climate for school reform that will last: Five critical factors. Catalyst for Change 30, no. 1: 11–13.

Hord, S. M. (1997). Professional learning communities: What are they and why are they important? Austin: Southwest Educational Development Laboratory. Retrieved from sdiplus.tie.wikispaces.net/.

Hord, S. M., W. Rutherford, L. Huling-Austin, and G. Gall. 1987. Taking charge of change. Alexandria, VA: Association for Supervision and Curriculum Development.

Kaplan, L. S., and W. A. Owings. 2013. Culture re-book: Reinvigorating school culture to improve student outcomes. Thousand Oaks, CA: Corwin Press.

Ladson-Billings, G. 1992. Reading between the lines and beyond the pages: A culturally relevant approach to literacy teaching. Theory into Practice, no. 31: 312–20.

Reyes, P., J. Scribner, and A. Paredes-Scribner. 1999. Lessons from high-performing Hispanic schools. New York: Teachers College Press.

Rosenthal, R., and L. Jacobsen. 1968. Pygmalion in the classroom. New York: Holt, Rinehart & Winston.

Schmoker, M. 1996. Results: The key to continuous school improvement. Alexandria, VA: Association for Supervision and Curriculum Development.

———. 2001. The results fieldbook. Alexandria, VA: Association for Supervision and Curriculum Development.

U.S. Census Bureau. 2012. USA quickfacts from the U.S. Census Bureau. Washington, DC: Author. Retrieved from quickfacts.census.go/qfd/states/00000.html.

Villegas, A. M., and T. Lucas. (2002). Educating culturally responsive teachers. Albany, NY: University of New York Press.

ADDITIONAL RESOURCES

Acker-Hocevar, M. A., J. Ballenger, A. W. Place, and G. Ivory (eds.). 2012. Snapshots of school leadership in the 21st century: The UCEA voices from the field project. Charlotte, NC: Information Age.

Acker-Hocevar, M. A., M. I. Cruz-Janzen, and C. L. Wilson. 2012. Leadership from the ground up: Effective schooling in traditionally low-performing schools. Charlotte, NC: Information Age.

Alford, B. J., and J. Ballenger. 2012. Leadership practices and processes that impact personnel, professional development, and teacher professionalism and influence school improvement. In Snapshots of school leadership in the 21st century: The UCEA voices from the field project (75–95). Edited by M. A. Acker-Hocevar, J. Ballenger, A. W. Place, and G. Ivory. Charlotte, NC: Information Age.

DuFour, R., and E. Robert. 1998. Professional learning communities at work: Best practices for enhancing student achievement. Alexandria, VA: Association for Supervision and Curriculum Development.

Fullan, M. 2008. The six secrets of change: What the best leaders do to help their organizations survive and thrive. San Francisco, CA: Jossey-Bass.

———. 2010. All systems go: The change imperative for whole system reform. Thousand Oaks, CA: Corwin Press.

———. 2010. Motion leadership: The skinny of becoming change savvy. Thousand Oaks, CA: Corwin Press.

Hipp, K. K., and J. B. Huffman. 2010. Demystifying professional learning communities: School leadership at its best. New York: Rowman & Littlefield Education.

Jenlink, P. M., and F. H. Townes. 2009. The struggle for identity in today's schools: Cultural recognition in a time of increasing diversity. New York: Rowman & Littlefield Education.

Kersten, T. A., and J. Ballenger. 2012. School and district relationships. In Snapshots of school leadership in the 21st century: The UCEA voices from the field project (75–95). Edited by M. A. Acker-Hocevar, J. Ballenger, A. W. Place, and G. Ivory. Charlotte, NC: Information Age.

Ladson-Billings, G. 2001. Crossing over to Canaan: The journey of new teachers in diverse classrooms. San Francisco: Jossey-Bass.

Lindsey, D. B., L. D. Jungwirth, J. V. N. C. Pahl, and R. B. Lindsey. 2009. Culturally proficient learning communities: Confronting inequities through collaborative curiosity. Thousand Oaks, CA: Corwin Press.

Lindsey, R. B., S. M. Graham, R. C. Westphal, and C. L. Jew. 2008. Culturally proficient inquiry: A lens for identifying and examining educational gaps. Thousand Oaks, CA: Corwin Press.

Papa, R., F. W. English. 2011. Turnaround principals for underperforming schools. New York: Rowman & Littlefield Education.

Reeves, D. 2009. Leading change in your school: How to conquer myths, build commitment, and get results. Alexandria, VA: Association for Supervision and Curriculum Development.

Shoho, A. R., B. G. Barnett, and A. L. Tooms (eds.). 2010. The challenges for new principals in the twenty-first century: Developing leadership capabilities through professional support. Charlotte, NC: Information Age.

Tileston, D. W., and S. K. Darling. 2008. Why culture counts: Teaching children of poverty. Bloomington, IN: Solution Tree.

Chapter Six

Grayson High School in Trouble

Texas Principal Exam Competency 006: The principal knows how to implement a staff evaluation and development system to improve the performance of all staff members, select and implement appropriate models for supervision and staff development, and apply the legal requirements for personnel management.

Texas Chapter 149 Standard 2 (2014): Human Capital. The principal is responsible for ensuring there are high-quality teachers and staff in every classroom and throughout the school.

Texas Chapter 149 Standard 5 (2014): Strategic Operations. The principal is responsible for implementing systems that align with the school's vision and improve the quality of instruction.

ELCC Standard 1 (2011): A building-level leader applies knowledge that promotes the success of every student by collaboratively facilitating the development, articulation, implementation, and stewardship of a shared school vision of learning through the collection and use of data to identify school goals, assess organizational effectiveness, and implement school plans to achieve school goals; promotion of continual and sustainable school improvement; and evaluation of school progress and revision of school plans supported by school-based stakeholders.

ABSTRACT

The principal of this school is faced with using the new state-mandated data assessment to create a campus plan that will benefit students. A part of this challenge centers on working with a faculty that is divided in its support of how best to use this information. At the same time, the local community is beginning to question the effectiveness of the high school based on the reports from the state assessment center.

OBJECTIVES

1. The principal implements daily schedules and a yearlong calendar that plans for regular data-driven instruction cycles, gives students access to diverse and rigorous course offerings, and builds in time for staff professional development.
2. Principals ensure that, once hired, teachers develop and grow by building layered supports that include regular observations, actionable feedback, and school-wide supports so that teachers know how they are performing.
3. Principals demonstrate the ability to optimize the learning environment for all students by applying appropriate models and principles of organizational development and management, including data-driven decision making with attention to indicators of equity, effectiveness, and efficiency.
4. Principals allocate appropriate time, funding, and other needed resources to ensure the effective implementation of campus and professional development plans.

LITERATURE REVIEW

Standardized Testing

In the twenty-first century, more and more decisions about students, teachers, administrators, and schools are based on the results of standardized tests. With the passage of state-mandated testing and the No Child Left Behind Act (NCLB) (2001), the United States continues to raise the bar of education, and the tensions of testing have become even more pronounced. Although NCLB received bipartisan support in Congress, it has become the subject of harsh criticism from both the political left and right. Ravitch (2010) posited that "the problem with using tests to make important decisions about people's lives is that standardized tests are not precise instruments" (349–50). While standardized tests have their place in assessing educational achievement, these tests should not be an end in itself (Ravitch 2010).

The Obama administration released its blueprint for revising the Elementary and Secondary Education Act (ESEA) in 2010. The blueprint eliminated the school rating system based on students' test scores and annual yearly progress and extended the 2014 proficiency deadline to 2020. While schools will still be measured against annual measurable objectives calculated and reported under NCLB, the new standards will recognize growth in performance and no longer rely on high-stakes testing (A Blueprint for Reform 2010).

Instructional Coaching

Instructional coaching has emerged as one of the more effective professional development models for adult learners, whereby teachers are provided one-on-one assistance based on their instructional needs (Williamson 2012). The principal often serves as evaluator and instructional coach. When serving in the role of an instructional coach, the role of evaluator should remain separate, and the principal should set clear boundaries about how information from coaching will be used. Good coaches share the following characteristics:

- Create an environment that welcomes teachers, in which coaching is not seen as a punishment or requirement.
- Help teachers identify goals for their teaching and support their efforts to improve.
- Listen intently to teachers and create a comfortable setting where the teacher can be open without fear of retribution.
- Ask thoughtful, open-ended questions that promote reflection.
- Use data from the observation or comments made by teachers to provide feedback. (Knight 2011, 18–22)

Needs Assessment

Before a principal can plan staff development, the needs of faculty and the needs of students must be identified. London and Wueste (1992) identified three basic methods principals used to determine the training needs of faculty:

- Reviewing performance appraisals (identifying faculty with performance below the acceptable standards who need training)
- Conducting organizational analyses (identifying grade levels with low student pass scores on standardized tests)
- Surveying human resources (interviewing faculty)

In addition to this, Findley (2002) suggested that informal needs assessments for staff development actually occur anytime that the faculty is together because opportunities for them to get to know one another better, lead to more specific, collaborative work efforts.

Identify Objectives

Objectives should be meaningful, concise, and measurable. These objectives usually fall into three categories:

- Transmitting information, such as orientation;
- Changing attitudes: a type of socialization that helps everyone in the school have a better understanding of its culture in order to be effective;
- Developing three kinds of skills: human skills, which increase leadership and teamwork; technical skills, which focus on specific functions, such as presenting information in the classroom; and conceptual skills, which are necessary for decision making that is integrated into the whole school system.

A benefit of focusing on particular objectives during the supervisory process is that it clarifies the monitoring process for the principal and helps teachers accomplish needed behavior changes (Whitaker 1999).

Selecting Training Methods

There are many methods to train and develop faculty, including orientation programs, workshops, behavior modeling, simulations, case discussions, conferencing, role playing, assigned readings, and faculty meetings (Bagin and Gallagher 2001). Issues to consider in selecting development methods include the objective of the training, the cost, the time involved, the number of participants, and the background of the individuals.

New Teacher and Principal Evaluation Systems

A shift has occurred in the way teachers and principals are evaluated. Under these new statewide evaluation systems, teachers and principals will be evaluated on measures of professional practices as well as student growth. The purpose of the Texas Principal Evaluation System is to assess principals' performance in relation to the Texas Principal Standards. The evaluation system will:

- serve as a measurement of leadership performance;
- guide leaders as they reflect upon and improve their effectiveness;
- focus the goals and objectives of schools and districts as they support, monitor, and evaluate their principals;
- guide professional development for principals;
- serve as a tool in developing coaching and mentoring programs for the principalship; and
- inform higher education programs in developing the content and requirements of degree programs that prepare future principals. (Texas Education Agency 2014a)

The new Texas Teacher Evaluation and Support System (T-TESS) was designed to support teachers in their professional development and help them grow and improve education. The statewide rollout is scheduled for the 2016–2017 school year. The T-TESS evaluation includes three measures, which are:

- Observation
- Teacher Self-Assessment
- Student Growth. (Texas Education Agency 2014b)

Data-Based Decision Making

Data-based decision making relies on the use of multiple measures of data to help inform leadership decisions. Principals create data leadership teams comprised of teachers, administrators, school instructional specialists, parents, and business leaders to analyze multiple types and sources of data to enhance school improvement. The purpose of the data leadership teams is to utilize data to improve the learning experiences of all students (Guthrie and Schuermann 2011).

When principals and leadership teams measure and analyze student data they are able to make sure that students do not fall through the cracks. Some of the measures and types of data may include demographics (i.e., enrollment, dropout rate, etc.); school processes (i.e., description of school programs and processes), student learning (i.e., standardized tests, teacher observation, authentic assessments), and perceptions (i.e., perceptions of attitudes, values, and the learning environment) (Bernhardt 2012).

Guthrie and Schuermann (2011) noted that using reliably collected data helps educators to lead schools to:

- Progress toward continuous student and organizational improvement;
- Focus on and establish priorities for instructional and staff development efforts and monitor individual and collective progress;
- Meet district, state, and federal accountability requirements; and
- Develop a sense of community through sustained, collective learning.

Data-Driven Leadership

Data-driven decision leadership is not all about data. Shared leadership, vision, and core values are critical to data-driven decision making (Bernhardt 2012). The core values that guide and help make sense of the data include: (a) ambitious standards for student learning; (b) belief in human capacity; (c) commitment to equity and equality; (d) belief in professional support and responsibility; and (e) commitment to inquiry (Knapp, Swinnerton, Copland, and Monpas-Huber 2006).

Professional Development and Standards

Guthrie and Schuermann (2010) defined professional development as "the sustained or continued education and in-service training of teachers, administrators and other professionals connected with schooling" (335). Quality professional development is a key factor in achieving change in schools. While hiring the right teachers is important, professional development is instrumental in school improvement efforts.

The Learning Forward (formerly National Staff Development Council), with the contribution of forty professional associations and education organizations, including the National Education Association (NEA), developed the Standards for Professional Learning. These standards for professional learning are designed to increase educator effectiveness and results for all students through the use of:

- Professional Learning Communities that use sources and types of student, educator, and system data to plan, assess, and evaluate professional learning;
- Skillful leaders who develop capacity, advocate, and create support systems for professional learning;
- Resources that are prioritized, monitored, and coordinated for educators' use;
- Data to plan, assess, and evaluate professional learning; and
- Learning Designs that integrate theories, research, and models of human learning (Learning Forward 2011).
- Implementation that applies research on change and sustains support for implementation of professional learning; and
- Outcomes that are aligned with education performance and student curriculum standards.

CASE STUDY

John Thomas, principal of Grayson High School, shook his head as he considered the day's events. He had started the day meeting with the faculty assigned to the new leadership data team. The purpose of today's meeting had been to review the reports from the state data-collecting system, the SAPR (State Academic Performance Report), in preparation for designing a campus plan for the upcoming school year. But what he had expected to be a collaborative time of planning had quickly dissolved into arguments and excuse making.

Principal Thomas overheard the newer teachers on the committee grumbling because they were not "paid enough to come in for these meetings." Then, when he began to explain the reporting system for the data, one of the oldest staff members had joked that all this "data-driven" planning was only driving them to one place—an early retirement. Although he laughed, he had seen the knowing looks that colleagues shared when she said this.

But the worst was yet to come. After working late in his office and mulling over the events of the meeting, he drove to his home. His wife met him at the door with a newspaper in her hand and a worried expression on her face. She handed him the newspaper, which was folded to the editorial page. He took the paper from her and read the following:

Grayson High School in Trouble

We have always been proud of Grayson High School, but now that the results of the new State Academic Performance Report are available for everyone in the community to review, we are shocked! Here are just a few of the surprising and very disappointing statistics that were reported:

	Year	Campus	African American	Hispanic	White
All Subjects	2013	44%	49%	57%	59%
	2012	71%	70%	71%	72%
Reading	2013	45%	40%	56%	55%
	2012	71%	71%	71%	88%
Mathematics	2013	42%	42%	53%	55%
	2012	71%	62%	72%	71%
Writing	2013	36%	31%	46%	42%
	2012	36%	48%	48%	50%

The State Test revealed a significant decrease from the 2012 to the 2013 school year in all subjects and in areas of reading, mathematics and writing for our student population.

In addition, the end-of-course exams revealed dismal results in the areas of Algebra 1, ELA Writing I and ELA Writing II:

2013	Campus	African American	Hispanic	White
Algebra 1	57%	41%	60%	78%
ELA Writing I	37%	30%	37%	67%
ELA Writing II	34%	32%	34%	39%

Grayson High School

Grayson High School had a good reputation in this growing suburban community that was located less than fifty miles from one of the ten largest cities in the United States. Many people said that they moved here because the reputation of the school was so good. Last year, the Chamber of Commerce had erected a sign at the outskirts of town advertising the benefits of the city, and right in the center was a picture of the high school.

While the extracurricular program centered on the boys' basketball team and the football team, the varsity cheerleaders regularly won the state National Cheerleader Association competitions. The student council was active, and parents were in and out of the building on a regular basis helping with bake sales to raise money for the band, pep club, and other activities. The community was diverse, with a large population of African American and Hispanic students. Within the past two years, a group of Islamic families had moved to the community from the Middle East. Several of the female students still wore a *burkha*, but for the most part these kids stayed to themselves and caused no trouble.

BENCHMARK TESTING

For years, the entire Grayson school system had been known throughout the state for its system of benchmark testing that tested students and placed them in classes based on this information. Up until last year, all students had been tested in core subjects—language arts, mathematics, science, and social studies—at the end of each nine-week instructional period. These benchmark tests were used to determine specific strengths and weaknesses of each student, and instruction was modified accordingly. Teachers, working in teams, had made most of the instructional decisions, including which students would attend after-school tutorials. Teachers and the community liked their system of doing things and had been disappointed when the state introduced the new testing program.

While results of the benchmark testing had never been published in the newspaper, they had always been available for any parent who had questions about their students' progress or placement. Now, not only was the new SAPR information in the newspaper, but the entire report for every school in the state was available on the Internet, accessible to anyone interested enough to take the time to seek out this information.

District Name: GRAYSONISD
Campus Name: Grayson H S

Total Students: 1,860
Grade Span: 09 - 12
School Type: High School

State EDUCATION AGENCY
State Academic Performance Report
2012-13 Campus Performance

STAAR Percent at Phase-in 1 Level II or Above End of Course

	Year	State	District	Campus	African American	Hispanic	White	American Indian	Asian	Pacific Islander	Two or More Races	Special Ed	Econ Disadv	ELL
ELA Reading I	2013	69%	57%	48%	40%	49%	59%	*	41%	*	*	39%	47%	33%
ELA Reading II	2013	79%	72%	66%	62%	68%	68%	*	*	*	-	30%	65%	50%
ELA Reading III	2013	83%	63%	*	*	*	*	-	-	-	-	*	*	*
Algebra I	2013	78%	67%	57%	41%	60%	78%	*	*	-	-	47%	55%	55%
Geometry	2013	85%	79%	74%	70%	75%	68%	*	56%	*	*	38%	75%	67%
Algebra II	2013	97%	96%	90%	100%	89%	100%	-	*	*	-	-	87%	88%
ELA Writing I	2013	55%	45%	37%	30%	37%	67%	*	33%	*	*	45%	35%	26%
ELA Writing II	2013	55%	44%	34%	32%	34%	39%	*	*	*	-	38%	33%	17%
Biology	2013	84%	78%	75%	59%	77%	87%	*	62%	*	*	46%	75%	67%
Chemistry	2013	84%	80%	76%	76%	76%	65%	*	86%	*	-	31%	77%	71%
World Geography	2013	75%	69%	67%	56%	68%	92%	+	64%	*	*	43%	66%	59%
World History	2013	71%	66%	64%	54%	65%	78%	*	71%	*	-	30%	62%	47%
U.S. History	2013	72%	62%	*	*	*	*	-	-	-	-	*	*	*
	66.1%	52.8%	48.0%	n/a	n/a	n/a	n/a	n/a	n/a	n/a	n/a	n/a	n/a	n/a

Figure 6.1.

District Name: GRAYSONISD
Campus Name: Grayson H S

Total Students: 1,860
Grade Span: 09 - 12
School Type: High School

State EDUCATION AGENCY
State Academic Performance Report
2012-13 Campus Performance

STAAR Percent at Phase-in 1 Level II or Above
All Grades

		State	District	Campus	African American	Hispanic	White	American Indian	Asian	Pacific Islander	Two or More Races	Special Ed	Econ Disadv	ELL
All Subjects	2013	77%	69%	44%	49%	57%	59%	54%	50%	74%	100%	46%	45%	41%
	2012	77%	67%	71%	70%	71%	72%	68%	63%	78%	*	49%	71%	51%
Reading	2013	80%	71%	45%	40%	56%	55%	*	49%	100%	*	42%	53%	43%
	2012	79%	69%	71%	71%	71%	88%	*	54%	*	*	58%	71%	45%
Mathematics	2013	79%	70%	42%	42%	53%	55%	*	62%	88%	*	46%	51%	61%
	2012	77%	65%	71%	62%	72%	71%	*	71%	*	*	42%	70%	55%
Writing	2013	63%	53%	36%	31%	46%	42%	*	35%	*	*	22%	24%	13%
	2012	67%	57%	36%	48%	48%	50%	*	*	*	-	45%	35%	19%
Science	2013	82%	75%	81%	73%	82%	85%	*	74%	100%	*	50%	80%	71%
	2012	80%	69%	81%	78%	82%	83%	71%	71%	*	*	45%	80%	64%
Social Studies	2013	76%	72%	75%	66%	75%	88%	*	79%	100%	*	50%	73%	61%
	2012	79%	74%	81%	79%	80%	86%	100%	76%	*	*	51%	81%	62%

Figure 6.1. *Continued.*

District Name: GRAYSON ISD
Campus Name: Grayson II S

State EDUCATION AGENCY
State Academic Performance Report
2012-13 Campus Profile

Total Students: 1,860
Grade Span: 09 - 12
School Type: High School

Student Information	Campus Count	Campus Percent	District	State
Total Students:	1,860	100.0%	158,680	5,058,939
Students by Grade:				
Early Childhood Education	0	0.0%	0.2%	0.3%
Pre-Kindergarten	0	0.0%	5.7%	4.5%
Kindergarten	0	0.0%	8.8%	7.7%
Grade 1	0	0.0%	8.9%	7.8%
Grade 2	0	0.0%	8.5%	7.7%
Grade 3	0	0.0%	8.1%	7.6%
Grade 4	0	0.0%	7.8%	7.5%
Grade 5	0	0.0%	7.6%	7.4%
Grade 6	0	0.0%	7.2%	7.5%
Grade 7	0	0.0%	6.7%	7.5%
Grade 8	0	0.0%	6.3%	7.2%
Grade 9	533	28.7%	7.2%	8.0%
Grade 10	509	27.4%	6.3%	6.9%
Grade 11	428	23.0%	5.4%	6.5%
Grade 12	390	21.0%	5.1%	6.0%
Ethnic Distribution:				
African American	287	15.4%	23.7%	12.7%
Hispanic	1,392	74.8%	69.4%	51.3%
White	98	5.3%	4.8%	30.0%
American Indian	12	0.6%	0.4%	0.4%
Asian	56	3.0%	1.2%	3.6%
Pacific Islander	9	0.5%	0.1%	0.1%
Two or More Races	6	0.3%	0.5%	1.8%
Economically Disadvantaged	1,470	79.0%	89.0%	60.4%
Non-Educationally Disadvantaged	390	21.0%	11.0%	39.6%
English Language Learners (ELL)	426	22.9%	39.5%	17.1%
Students w/ Disciplinary Placements (2011-2012)	36	1.7%	1.4%	1.7%
At-Risk	1,219	65.5%	59.9%	44.7%
Mobility (2011-2012)	454	21.7%	22.4%	17.9%
Graduates (Class of 2012):				
Total Graduates	327	100.0%	7,275	292,636
By Ethnicity (incl. Special Ed.):				
African American	58	17.7%	2,072	38,213
Hispanic	224	68.5%	4,547	131,106
White	30	9.2%	465	105,767
American Indian	2	0.6%	68	1,427
Asian	11	3.4%	93	10,871
Pacific Islander	2	0.6%	3	396
Two or More Races	0	0.0%	27	4,856
By Graduation Type (incl. Special Ed.):				
Minimum H.S. Program	48	14.7%	1,108	57,010
Recommended H.S. Program/DAP	279	85.3%	6,167	235,626
Special Education Graduates	30	9.2%	611	25,213

Figure 6.1. *Continued.*

State EDUCATION AGENCY
State Academic Performance Report
2012-13 Campus Profile

District Name: GRAYSON ISD
Campus Name: Grayson H S

Total Students: 1,860
Grade Span: 09 - 12
School Type: High School

Class Size Information

	Campus	District	State
Class Size Averages by Grade and Subject (Derived from teacher responsibility records):			
Elementary:			
Kindergarten	-	19.3	19.6
Grade 1	-	19.8	19.5
Grade 2	-	18.9	19.4
Grade 3	-	18.6	19.3
Grade 4	-	18.6	19.5
Grade 5	-	19.7	21.4
Grade 6	-	17.3	21.1
Mixed Grades	-	15.0	24.6
Secondary:			
English/Language Arts	15.9	16.7	17.4
Foreign Languages	19.4	16.0	19.0
Mathematics	19.6	17.0	18.0
Science	17.8	18.4	19.0
Social Studies	17.7	18.0	19.7

Figure 6.1. *Continued.*

District Name: GRAYSON ISD
Campus Name: Grayson H S

State EDUCATION AGENCY
State **Academic Performance Report**
2012-13 Campus Profile

Total Students: 1,860
Grade Span: 09 - 12
School Type: High School

Staff Information	Campus		District	State
	Count/Average	Percent		
Total Staff	136.5	100.0%	100.0%	100.0%
Professional Staff:	123.7	90.6%	70.0%	63.9%
Teachers	109.1	79.9%	55.0%	51.0%
Professional Support	8.0	5.9%	10.8%	9.0%
Campus Administration (School Leadership)	6.6	4.8%	3.4%	2.9%
Educational Aides:	12.9	9.4%	9.4%	9.3%
Total Minority Staff:	67.7	49.6%	72.0%	45.1%
Teachers by Ethnicity and Sex:				
African American	29.0	26.6%	37.3%	9.4%
Hispanic	12.1	11.1%	26.6%	24.9%
White	59.8	54.8%	31.2%	62.8%
American Indian	1.0	0.9%	0.3%	0.4%
Asian	5.2	4.8%	2.4%	1.4%
Pacific Islander	0.0	0.0%	0.1%	0.1%
Two or More Races	2.0	1.8%	2.0%	1.1%
Males	55.8	51.1%	29.0%	23.2%
Females	53.3	48.9%	71.0%	76.8%
Teachers by Years of Experience:				
Beginning Teachers	11.0	10.1%	8.9%	7.0%
1-5 Years Experience	28.6	26.2%	27.5%	26.1%
6-10 Years Experience	30.3	27.8%	22.3%	22.7%
11-20 Years Experience	22.6	20.7%	24.2%	26.9%
Over 20 Years Experience	16.6	15.2%	17.1%	17.3%
Number of Students per Teacher	17.0	n/a	16.0	15.5

Figure 6.1. *Continued.*

State EDUCATION AGENCY
State Academic Performance Report
2012-13 Campus Profile

District Name: GRAYSON ISD
Campus Name: Grayson H S

Total Students: 1,860
Grade Span: 09 - 12
School Type: High School

Staff Information

	Campus	District	State
Average Years Experience of Teachers:	10.4	11.4	11.5
Average Years Experience of Teachers with District:	7.9	9.1	8.0
Average Teacher Salary by Years of Experience (regular duties only):			
Beginning Teachers	$45,100	$46,740	$41,878
1-5 Years Experience	$47,199	$47,586	$44,354
6-10 Years Experience	$50,355	$49,964	$46,784
11-20 Years Experience	$55,966	$54,971	$50,587
Over 20 Years Experience	$62,254	$64,697	$58,291
Average Actual Salaries (regular duties only):			
Teachers	$51,968	$52,755	$48,821
Professional Support	$65,736	$62,988	$57,253
Campus Administration (School Leadership)	$78,128	$74,703	$71,259
Instructional Staff Percent:	n/a	69.0%	64.2%
Contracted Instructional Staff (not incl. above):	0.0	0.0	1,556.8

Program Information

	Campus Count	Campus Percent	District	State
Student Enrollment by Program:				
Bilingual/ESL Education	374	20.1%	36.9%	16.6%
Career & Technical Education	1,239	66.6%	20.3%	22.0%
Gifted & Talented Education	141	7.6%	11.7%	7.7%
Special Education	188	10.1%	7.4%	8.5%
Teachers by Program (population served):				
Bilingual/ESL Education	6.3	5.8%	2.6%	5.3%
Career & Technical Education	9.6	8.8%	3.4%	4.1%
Compensatory Education	0.0	0.0%	0.0%	2.9%
Gifted & Talented Education	0.1	0.1%	1.1%	2.0%
Regular Education	61.1	56.0%	78.6%	73.2%
Special Education	17.3	15.9%	10.1%	9.2%
Other	14.6	13.4%	4.3%	3.3%

Figure 6.1. *Continued.*

The New SAPR

The state board of education emphasized that the availability of information from the new SAPR reports would make it much easier for schools to understand the needs of their students. Testing results would support staff planning, improved supervision of teachers, and more learning for students much more effectively than the old testing information, which mostly had been left to individual school districts. In fact, "data-driven decision making" was a common phrase that was supported throughout education. While most educators agreed that data would be helpful in making decisions, not everyone agreed that the state's standardized testing was the best way to gather information about students. And, even if they did agree, they just did not know what to do with all these data. Principal Thomas had not anticipated the level of emotions that the new testing and its results would generate. (See figure 6.1.)

DISCUSSION QUESTIONS

1. If you were the principal, what would you consider the priority issues in this case?
2. Divide into small groups and role-play the following scenarios:

   a. The principal meets with a teacher who does not support the new testing system.
   b. The principal meets with an angry parent who is concerned after reading the editorial that her child is not being taken care of by the school system.
   c. The principal meets with the editor of the school newspaper to discuss the editorial.
   d. The principal meets with the superintendent to present the campus plan created by the faculty based on the SAPR scores.

3. Use the information provided in figure 6.1 and discuss implications presented by the data regarding student pass rate on the SAPR, teacher information, and the campus budget.
4. Obtain a copy of your school's campus plan and your school's testing report. Evaluate the plan based on the test report.
5. Use the information provided in figure 6.1 to create a comprehensive campus plan for the school in the case. Include in your plan, goals,

objectives, specific actions to be taken, evaluation, timeline, and resources. Prioritize the elements of the campus plan.

6. Based on the campus plan created in question 5, outline professional development needs for your campus that specifically address curriculum and instructional needs of teachers as identified in the SAPR.

7. Conduct an assessment of a staff development activity that was held at your school recently. Discuss several ways that these data could be gathered.

8. In reviewing the campus report in figure 6.1, identify a problem that needs to be studied immediately. Write a problem statement and research questions that will guide the study.

9. Design a simple study to collect data that will provide the school with additional information on the problem. How will you collect data? What kind of data will you collect? How will data be analyzed?

10. Divide the class into two groups and debate the issue of mandating national standards.

ON YOUR OWN—CONSIDER

Earl Smith, principal of Lone Star High School, discovered that while the school had enjoyed a reputation for outstanding student achievement over the years, there had been a subtle drop in test scores for African American and Hispanic student populations.

Earl convened a series of meeting with the Data Leadership team in which they discussed data to illustrate the need for higher student achievement for the African American and Hispanic students. The team members discussed ideas about revamping the school's traditional curriculum to make it more culturally relevant for these student populations.

After several meetings with the Data Leadership team, faculty representative Michelle Roth suggested to Earl that teachers should focus on teaching for the tests. "We will surely get results if we focus on what the tests require," she stated confidently. In addition to Michelle's comments, individual teachers spoke of their own concerns about the school's performance.

John Holton bluntly stated, "We have good teachers here but we can't get the results we want because the community and the parents do not give us the support we need." Another teacher commented, "These students have so many emotional needs we must respond to before we can teach the academics. I wish the tests would measure the dedication and the love we give to our students. These tests are no way to judge a school."

Frank Jones tried to help Earl with his own interpretation of the pressure to get better results. "Everything runs in cycles, Earl. This too shall pass. We are doing the best we can with limited resources. We have heavy turnover of teachers every year and it takes time to bring the new staff up to speed," said Frank.

What steps should the principal take to support students and faculty?

REMEMBER

A building-level leader applies knowledge that promotes the success of every student through the collection and use of data to identify school goals, assess organizational effectiveness, and implement school plans to achieve school goals.

REFERENCES

Bagin, D., and D. Gallagher. 2001. The school and community relations. 7th ed. Boston: Allyn & Bacon.

Bernhardt, V. L. 2012. Data analysis for continuous improvement. 3rd ed. Larchmont, NY: Eye on Education.

Blueprint for reform: The reauthorization of the Elementary and Secondary Education Act. 2010. United States Department of Education, Office of Planning, Evaluation and Policy Development, Washington, DC. Retrieved from www.ed.gov/policy/elsec/leg/blueprint/publication.html.

Findley, B. 2002. Needs-driven staff development. Principal Leadership 2, no. 7: 17–19.

Guthrie, J. W., and P. J. Schuermann, 2011. Successful school leadership: Planning, politics, performance, and power. Boston: Allyn & Bacon.

Knapp, M. S., J. A. Swinnerton, M. A. Copland, and J. Monpas-Huber. 2006. Data-informed leadership in education. Center for the Study of Teaching and Policy, Seattle, WA: University of Washington.

Knight, J. 2011. Coaching: The new leadership skills: What good coaches do. Educational Leadership 69, no. 2: 18–22.

Learning Forward. 2011. Standards for professional learning. Retrieved from www.learningforward.org.

London, M., and R. A. Wueste. 1992. Human resource development in changing organizations. Westport, CT: Greenwood.

Ravitch, D. 2010. The death and life of the great American school system: How testing and choice are undermining education. New York: Basic Books. Retrieved www.perseusbooks.com.

Texas Education Agency. 2014a. Texas principal evaluation system: User's guide. McREL International. Retrieved from tea.texas.go/workarea/linkit.

————. 2014b. Texas teacher evaluation and support system. Retrieved from tea.texas.gov/Texas-Educators/Educator-Evaluation-and-Support-system/Texas-Teacher-Evaluation-and-Support-System.

Williamson, R. 2012. Coaching teachers: An important principal role. Education Partnerships. Retrieved from www.educationpartnerships.org.

ADDITIONAL RESOURCES

Bellamy, G. T., C. L. Fulmer, M. J. Murphy, and R. Muth. 2007. Principal accomplishment: How school leaders succeed. New York: Teachers College Press.

English, F. W. 2008. Anatomy of professional practice: Promising research perspectives on educational leadership. New York: Rowman & Littlefield Education.

Firestone, W. A., and C. Riehl (eds.) 2005. A new agenda for research in educational leadership. New York: Teachers College Press.

Leithwood, K., S. Reid, L. Pedwell, and M. Connor. 2011. Lessons about improving leadership on a large scale: From Ontario's leadership strategy. In The international handbook of leadership for learning (335–52). Edited by T. Townsend and J. MacBeath. New York: Springer.

Murphy, J. 2004. Leadership for literacy: Research-based practice, PreK–3. Thousand Oaks, CA: Corwin Press.

Papa, R., and F. W. English. 2011. Turnaround principals for underperforming schools. New York: Rowman & Littlefield Education.

Pisapia, J. 2009. The strategic leader. Charlotte, NC: Information Age.

Reitzug, U., and D. West. 2011. A developmental framework for instructional leadership. In The international handbook of leadership for learning (169–88). Edited by T. Townsend and J. MacBeath. New York: Springer.

Rubin, H. 2002. Collaborative leadership: Developing effective partnerships in communities and schools. Thousand Oaks, CA: Corwin Press.

Willamson, R., and B. R. Blackburn. 2009. The principalship from A to Z. Larchmont, NY: Eye on Education.

Chapter Seven

No One Is College Bound Here

Texas Principal Exam Competency 007: The principal knows how to apply organizational decision-making and problem-solving skills to ensure an effective learning environment.

TAC Standard 1 (2014): Instructional Leadership. The principal is responsible for ensuring every student receives high-quality instruction.

TAC Standard 5 (2014): Strategic Operations. The principal is responsible for implementing systems that align with the school's vision and improve the quality of instruction.

ELCC Standard 6.0 (2011): A building-level education leader applies knowledge that promotes the success of every student by understanding, responding to, and influencing the larger political, social, economic, legal, and cultural context through advocating for school students, families, and caregivers; acting to influence local, district, state, and national decisions affecting student learning in a school environment; and anticipating and assessing emerging trends and initiatives in order to adapt school-based leadership strategies.

ABSTRACT

This case involves a high school in a low socioeconomic rural area that has a limited curriculum. Very few students go to college when they graduate. Those who do go to college, according to the nearby community college, do not do well. The principal has a desire to turn this high school around, but attitudes of teachers and parents create a barrier.

OBJECTIVES

Principals know how to analyze the complex causes of poverty and other disadvantages and their effects on families, communities, children, and learning.

1. Principals demonstrate the ability to analyze and describe the economic factors shaping a local community and the effects that economic factors have on local schools.
2. Principals can describe the community norms and values and how they relate to the role of the school in promoting social justice.
3. Principals demonstrate the ability to communicate with members of a school community concerning trends, issues, and potential changes in the environment in which the school operates, including maintenance of an ongoing dialogue with representatives of diverse community groups.
4. Principals frame, analyze, and resolve problems using appropriate problem-solving techniques and decision-making skills.

LITERATURE REVIEW

A postsecondary education offers numerous benefits to workers including higher earnings, lower rates of unemployment, and greater civic engagement (Long 2014). However, without a degree, the American workforce will not have the knowledge and skills needed to be successful in today's global economy (McKiernan 2012). Consequently, the U.S. economy and the twenty-first-century workforce have demanded more college-degreed workers (Carnevale, Smith, and Strohl 2010).

McCabe and Day (1998) noted that in 1950, 80 percent of jobs were classified as "unskilled." By 2018, the United States will have 46.8 million job openings and 30 million of these jobs will require some kind of postsecondary education (Carnevale, Smith, and Strolh 2012). However, access to higher education still remains a barrier for many families.

Barriers

In 2010 approximately 82 percent of students from high-income families attended college in comparison to only 52 percent of students from low-income families (Long 2014). In addition to income, Long identified college and career readiness as an equally challenging barrier to postsecondary education. Students are required to pass academic placement tests to show evidence of their college readiness. Those who do not pass are placed into remedial or developmental courses, indicating that high school graduates are often not academically prepared for college. While academic preparation is a problem for many students, it is a problem that especially affects low-income and minority students. For example, 62 percent of white students graduate with four-year degrees, but only 50 percent of Hispanic and 40 percent of African-American students obtain their four-year degree (Aud, Hussar, Johnson, Kena, Roth, and Manning 2012). Often issues of social justice define these gaps.

Social Justice

Social justice signifies responsibility for ensuring equal opportunity for success for everyone. Unfortunately educators are not preparing students, especially low socioeconomic and minority students, for the changes in their world (Reinventing 2010). Dewey (1916) suggested that as educators influence what and how society learns, the world is continually constructed and reconstructed. Yet attitudes of leadership today often are embedded with a "privileged perspective which largely ignores issues of status, gender, and race" (Gosetti and Rusch 1995, 12).

Often, openmindedness, tolerance, and justice are not promoted, resulting in leadership attitudes that continually sustain inequity through stratifying groups of people (Rusch 2002). In order for issues of power and privilege to lead to a more just and equitable understanding of educational leadership, today's administrators are challenged to create a vision for their schools founded on moral and spiritual attitudes, language, and practices that understand and include words such as "compassion," "forgiveness," "wisdom," and "humility" (Beck and Foster 1999; Tillman 2002).

Relatedly, Dantley (2001) challenged educational leaders to consider three principles posited by West (1988)—deep-seated moralism, inescapable opportunism, and aggressive pessimism—as spiritual concepts that can change the embedded assumptions and behaviors of all involved.

Dantley (2001) refers to deep-seated moralism as principled leadership, which manifests itself in a careful and critical reflection of one's position on issues of justice, democracy, and fairness. Inescapable opportunism, which Dantley calls pragmatic leadership, challenges leaders to consciously consider the contradictions of spoken philosophies of democratic schools and the realities facing our schools. Profound pessimism leads to Dantley's idea of purposive leadership, which is focused on transforming schools. In other words, principals and other education leaders must reflect on where they stand regarding social justice, they must question the disconnect that exists between what we say and what we do, and finally, they must consider how schools can be transformed into places where social justice abounds.

Making Our Schools More Just

Apple (1999) noted that throughout the United States many contradictory proposals have been offered to make our schools more just. Some of these "fixes" have suggested greater forms of governmental control, especially considering equity and the oppressed. Hirsch (1999) suggested that the school should use a common curriculum in order to eliminate the extremes of wealth and poverty.

In 2010 the National Governors Association Center for Best Practices and the Council of Chief State School Officers, recognizing the value of authentic, real-life learning and rigorous curriculum, launched the Common Core, a combination of college and career readiness and K–12 standards to ensure all students would graduate from high school prepared for college, career, and life (Understand n.d.). Mayer (2001) challenged teachers to incorporate visual thinking and the graphic process into the classroom in order to create a climate where there is little failure.

Marzano, Pickering, and Pollock (2001) reported that the use of graphic processes resulted in a 27 percentile gain in academic achievement. Haycock (2001) argued that a rigorous curriculum must be available to all students. In 2004 the American Diploma Project developed a set of benchmarks to align high school standards and assessments with the knowledge and skills required for the demands of college and careers. This alignment necessitated a rigorous curriculum that would prepare all students for success, no matter the route they chose after graduation.

Lin (2001) emphasized the fundamental characteristic of caring, because when people sincerely care, they find ways to be just, fair, and equitable. Therefore, as the population in the United States becomes more diverse, school curricula must address multicultural education with the understanding that it is meant to help all students academically and socially (McCray and Beachum 2014).

Team and a Strategy for Change

In order to achieve common goals and bring about needed changes among the school community, people must learn to work together. However, school improvement requires change. Therefore, school leaders must be able to nurture and sustain change for improvements to be lasting (Harris 2006). In fact, Fullan (2001) emphasized that without the support and commitment of the faculty and the larger school community, change does not result in lasting improvements. This has led to the notion of distributed leadership which has become an important concept for today's leaders, although some consider distributed leadership just a more recent label for "shared leadership" or "transformational leadership" (Cordeiro and Cunningham 2013).

Spillane's (2006) model of distributed leadership uses a group of individuals to work together as a team. Thus, administrators, teacher leaders, site councils, and others work together to share responsibilities. Improving how a team works together means better performance for the entire school. It is important for teams to develop skills that include understanding the group role and stages of group development, leading in small groups, building trust, communicating effectively, problem solving, decision making, planning, conducting meetings, resolving conflict, and evaluating the group process (Maeroff 1993).

Structural organization development approaches typically involve group strategies to bring about change. An important component to consider is strategic planning, which allows an organization to look closely at the environment and anticipate issues that create barriers or opportunities for goal achievement. Strategic planning is more than just long-range planning, according to Lunenburg (1995), because it goes beyond basic planning procedures with the specific goal of transforming organizations.

Before principals can lead a school to accept change, they must consider reducing resistance to change which is inevitable in organizations. A seminal strategy that makes this more understandable, force-field analysis, was developed by Lewin (1951). This approach views an organization's status quo as a state of equilibrium that results from balancing two opposing forces: forces for change (driving forces) and forces opposed (restraining forces). When there is equilibrium, these two forces are in balance, and there is no change. Lewin (1951) considered a three-step change strategy for organizations and teams to use in bringing about change:

1. Breaking the equilibrium, or unfreezing the organization, happens when the forces that act to keep the organization in its current balance are reduced (for example, a shift in school population, increased drop-out rate, or passage of a new legislative requirement).
2. Moving involves developing new values and behaviors that change the structure of the organization.
3. Refreezing involves stabilizing the change and forming a new equilibrium. Principals who empower the faculty team to recognize and understand the forces that are inherent in change are likely to reduce much of the resistance to change.

CASE STUDY

Principal Andy Rogers was disappointed to hear the counselor from King Community College (KCC), John Jones, say that Landon High School (LHS) graduates were not prepared for college. Jones went on to say that very few of the LHS seniors enrolled at the community college, and when they did, they struggled and rarely finished the two-year program.

LHS is located less than fifty miles away from KCC, which is the closest college. The high school is in a rural community within seventy-five miles of a large urban city in the South. In addition to KCC, there are three four-year colleges within a hundred-mile radius of LHS. The population of the high school is 66 percent white, 20 percent African American, and 14 percent Hispanic. Few of the children who attend LHS have parents who graduated from college. In fact, a few years ago, a survey reported that nearly 50 percent of LHS parents did not even have a high school diploma. As a result, the school has a high ratio of students coming from low socioeconomic homes.

However, the demographics of this small town are beginning to change. Within the past few years, young professionals have been buying land and building homes to raise their families away from the city in the quiet of this rural community. There has been talk of building a Wal-Mart distribution plant nearby. Another company has recently bought a large tract of land to build a housing community with homes that start at $150,000. This will have a good effect on the economy of the community, so there is much local excitement.

Principal Rogers Reflects

As Rogers reflected on his meeting with the counselor, he found himself thinking about the curriculum at LHS. This was only his second year at the school, but last year, as a new principal, he had suggested that the school partner with the nearby community college to begin an Early College High School (ECHS). However, several department team leaders, all of whom had been at the high school for at least fifteen years, talked him out of this idea, saying that it "wouldn't fly" here. He remembered how disappointed he had been at the end of his first year when he saw the dwindling enrollment in college preparatory courses. He had been especially sorry to see that the calculus class, which was offered for the first time, had to be canceled because of low interest. He wondered now whether the problem was low interest or whether the students really had not been adequately prepared.

The school was also lacking in technology equipment. Last year he and one of the teachers had written a small grant that, when funded, allowed the high school to purchase twenty-five new computers. Prior to this, the computer lab at the high school had been used primarily to teach keyboarding. He remembered the excitement of the students when the new lab opened. Several students had come by his office, asking whether it could be opened after school.

The equipment in the chemistry lab and the biology lab was minimal. Teachers still relied heavily on lectures and implemented very few hands-on activities. Funding was always a problem, and there never seemed to be enough money to provide the labs with all that was needed for the science classes. Now he wondered whether teachers would use these resources if they had them—perhaps that was the problem. Regardless, he was beginning to understand why the students were not interested in taking some of these classes.

In addition to his concerns about the curriculum and the lack of equipment at the school, Rogers had other concerns, not the least of which was that KCC would go public with this complaint. That would be really bad, especially now that the community was beginning to get excited about new economic prospects. New families would certainly be interested in good schools.

Faculty Meeting

A week later, Rogers spoke at the faculty meeting. He told teachers about the meeting and pointed out that the college leadership was concerned that faculty at LHS were not doing an adequate job of preparing students for college and certainly not for KCC.

The teachers' reactions were varied. Many teachers pointed out that "these students are not interested in going to college anyway." This prompted an argument when other teachers stated that the students did want to go to college but could not afford it, not even KCC, which was so close. Others noted that the students had very little support from their families since few of them had gone to college themselves.

Some teachers thought that the report was exaggerated and felt sure that there were LHS graduates who went to KCC. If they did not do well, it was "probably because they got too involved in partying." Another commented that students were so busy working that college just did not seem necessary; after all, nearly all the students in the high school already held part-time jobs somewhere to help the family.

Finally, after listening to the different teacher comments, the principal handed out the State Accountability Assessment System Comparison Group Campus information (table 7.1). This reported the college-bound data for schools that are similar to LHS in size and demographics.

Table 7.1. State Accountability Assessment System (SAAS) Comparison Group Campus

High School	Total Grads	College-Bound
Barton	137	90
Appleland	206	21
Kindley	250	197
Gainville	141	100
Connally	156	102
Woden	388	216
Cosby	232	198
Landon	146	35
Henders	247	154
Coffey	149	78

Then the principal asked the faculty a question: "What can we do to see that more students who graduate from Landon High School go on to college?"

DISCUSSION QUESTIONS

1. How would you answer the principal's question?

2. Identify other issues that are related to this case. Select one issue from your list and frame the problem with possible solutions.

3. Using a decision-making technique, such as a force-field analysis, predict the needs of the community over the next five years.

4. Consider your findings. What impact will this have on the high school and its requirements for graduation?

5. How can the high school influence parents to encourage their children to go to college?

6. Design a strategy to help teachers and the local community to become student advocates for success.

7. Based on the information given in the case, construct a profile of a typical graduating senior. Consider political, economic, cultural, and social issues.

8. Develop a strategic plan that addresses specific issues to change student and teacher attitudes about the learning environment.

9. How would you ensure equity of funds and resources to change the climate of this school?

10. Compare this school with the high school in your community regarding issues of social justice. Consider the cultural context, curriculum offerings, and equity of funding.

ON YOUR OWN—CONSIDER

West Hills ISD has a student body of 1600, 36 percent are white, 48 percent are Hispanic, and 16 percent are African-American. Ninety-two percent of the students receive free or reduced lunch. The district hired a new superintendent for the 2014–2015 school year and during the summer a new homework policy was instituted at the high school. The new superintendent, Dr. Brown, believes that without a significant amount of homework, students cannot be successful. Homework would be required four nights a week for high school students and would count for 40 percent of the students' grades.

Janet, an eleventh grader with great potential, always excelled in her English classes. She always scored above average on her exams and assignments completed in class. Janet is Hispanic and eligible for free/reduced lunch. With the new homework policy, Janet's English III teacher, Ms. Corley, could not understand why she did not turn in homework. Wondering whether there was an issue at home, Ms. Corley has touched base several times with her colleagues who have Janet's younger siblings in their classes to see whether they were noticing similar patterns. She learned, on the contrary, that her younger siblings always turn in their homework.

Ms. Corley has reached out to Janet every way she knows how, from pleading with her to offering to give her more advanced work that might engage her in new ways. On several occasions she has asked Janet why she rarely turns in her homework. Each time, she received the same response: "I'll do it next time. I promise."

As a conscientious teacher, Ms. Corley wants to support Janet and to ensure her continued success. On the other hand, Ms. Corley knows that the homework-grading policy is clear: Students are allowed to turn in one homework assignment one day late without penalty—she calls this her "life happens" rule; but in every other instance, failure to turn in homework results in a grade of zero for that assignment. Ms. Corley makes an appointment with Ms. Grimes, the high school principal, to try to find out more information about Janet.

One day after school Ms. Grimes approaches Janet again about her homework and learns why she is not doing her homework. Janet's father finally found a steady job at the local mill. He works the night shift. When Janet's baby brother was born six months ago, her mother left and no one knows where she is. The dad takes care of the baby until Janet comes home from school. From the moment she gets home from school until her dad returns from work at 6:00 a.m., she is babysitting her five younger siblings. She is busy taking them to the playground, cooking them dinner, helping them with *their* homework. Ms. Corley now understands why Janet's siblings are able to complete their homework, but Janet is not. She shares this information with Ms. Grimes.

Ms. Grimes knows that there is no simple answer to this issue. She has approached Dr. Brown on several occasions regarding the district homework policy, but he is not willing to make any changes. What is the next step for this principal? How should the faculty and community be involved in the process of establishing policies for the district?

REMEMBER

The principal applies organizational decision-making and problem-solving skills to ensure an effective learning environment for all students.

REFERENCES

Apple, M. 1999. Teacher assessment ignores social injustice. Education Digest 65, no. 2: 24–28.

Aud, S., W. Hussar, F. Johnson, G. Kena, E. Roth, and E. Manning. 2012. A closer look at high school students in the United States over the last 20 years. nces.ed.gov/programs/coe/analysis/2012-section6.asp.

Beck, L., and W. Foster. 1999. Administration and community: Considering challenges, exploring possibilities. In Handbook of research on educational administration (337–58). 2nd ed. Edited by J. Murphy and K. Louis. San Francisco: Jossey-Bass.

Carnevale, A., N. Smith, and J. Strohl. (2010). Help wanted: Projections of jobs and education requirements through 2018. Washington, DC: Georgetown University Center on Education and the Workforce. Retrieved from cew.georgetown.edu/jobs2018/.

Cordeiro, P., and W. Cunningham. 2013. Educational leadership: A bridge to improved practice. Boston: Pearson.

Dantley, M. 2001. Transforming school leadership through Cornel West's notions of African American prophetic spirituality. Paper presented at the University Council for Educational Administration, Albuquerque, New Mexico, November.

Dewey, T. 1916. Democracy and education. New York: Macmillan.

Fullan, M. 2001. Leading in a culture of change. San Francisco: Jossey-Bass.

Gosetti, P., and E. Rusch. 1995. Re-examining educational leadership: Challenging assumptions. In Women leading in education (11–35). Edited by D. Dunlap and P. Schmuck. New York: State University of New York Press.

Harris, S. 2006. Best practices of award-winning secondary school principals. Thousand Oaks, CA: Corwin Press.

Haycock, K. 2001. Closing the achievement gap. Educational Leadership 58, no. 6: 6–11.

Hirsch, E. D. 1999. Americanization and the schools. Clearing House 72, no. 3: 136–39.

Lewin, K. 1951. Field theory in social sciences. New York: Harper & Row.

Lin, Q. 2001. Toward a caring-centered multicultural education within the social justice context. Education 1: 107–14.

Long, B. 2014. Proposal 6: Addressing the Academic Barriers to Higher Education. Brookings Institute. Retrieved from www.brookings.edu/search?start=1&q=Proposal 6.

Maeroff, G. 1993. Team building for school change: Equipping teachers for new roles. New York: Teachers College Press.

Marzano, R., J. Pickering, and J. Pollock. 2001. Classroom instruction that works: Research-based strategies for increasing student achievement. Alexandria VA: Association for Supervision and Curriculum Development.

Mayer, D. 2001. Social justice and the class community: Opening the door to possibilities. Educational Journal 90: 107–14.

McCabe, R., and Day, P. (eds). 1998. Development education: A twenty-first century and scoial economic imperative. Mission Viejo, CA: League for Innovation in the Community College.

McCray, C. R., and F. D. Beachum. 2014. School leadership in a diverse society. Charlotte, NC: Information Age.

McKiernan, H. 2002. Higher education and the American workforce. Trusteeship (20)3.

Rebore, R. 2003. A human relations approach to the practice of educational leadership. Boston: Allyn & Bacon.

Reinventing the federal role in education: Supporting the goal of college and career readiness for all students. 2010. Education Digest 75, no. 6: 34–43.

Rusch, E. 2002. The (un)changing world of school leadership: A journey from discourse to practice. In The changing world of school administration (60–79). Edited by G. Perreault and F. Lunenburg. Lanham, MD: Scarecrow Education.

Spillane, J. 2006. Distributed leadership. San Francisco: Jossey-Bass.

Tillman, L. 2002. The impact of diversity in educational administration. In The changing world of school administration (144–56). Edited by G. Perreault and F. Lunenburg. Lanham, MD: Scarecrow Education.

Understand how the common core was developed. n.d. Retrieved from www.corestandards .org/.

West, C. 1988. Prophetic fragments. Grand Rapids, MI: African World Press.

ADDITIONAL RESOURCES

Covey, S. 1990. Principle-centered leadership. New York: Simon & Schuster.

Drucker, P. 1993. Managing in turbulent times. New York: HarperCollins.

Foster, W. 1986. Paradigms and promises. Buffalo, NY: Prometheus.

Fullan, M., and A. Hargreaves. 1996. What's worth fighting for in your school. New York: Teachers College Press.

Lambert, L. 1998. Building leadership capacity in schools. Alexandria, VA: Association for Supervision and Curriculum Development.

———. 2002. Leadership as a form of learning: Implications for theory and practice. In The changing world of school administration. Edited by G. Perreault and F. Lunenburg. Lanham, MD: Scarecrow Education.

Organisation for Economic Co-operation and Development (OECD). 2014. Education at a glance 2014: OECD indicators. OECD Publishing. dx.doi.org/10.1787/eag-2014-en.

Palestrini, R. 1999. Educational administration: Leading with mind and heart. Lancaster, PA: Technomic.

Sarason, S. 2002. A call for professional-organizational self-scrutiny. In The changing world of school administration (131–43). Edited by G. Perreault and F. Lunenburg. Lanham, MD: Scarecrow Education.

Schumaker, D., and W. Sommers.2001. Being a successful principal: Riding the wave of change without drowning. Thousand Oaks, CA: Corwin Press.

Vroom, V., and A. Jago. 1988. The new leadership: Managing participation in organizations. Englewood Cliffs, NJ: Prentice Hall.

Whitaker, T. 1999. Dealing with difficult teachers. Larchmont, NY: Eye on Education.

Yukl, G. 1994. Leadership in organizations. 5th ed. Englewood Cliffs, NJ: Prentice Hall.

Chapter Eight

Politics or Sacred Cows

Texas Principal Exam Competency 008: The principal knows how to apply principles of effective leadership and management in relation to campus budgeting, personnel, resource utilization, financial management, and technology use.

TAC Standard 3 (2014): Executive Leadership. The principal is responsible for modeling a consistent focus on and commitment to improving student learning.

ELCC Standard 3 (2011): A building-level education leader applies knowledge that promotes the success of every student by ensuring the management of the school organization, operation, and resources through monitoring and evaluating the school management and operational systems; efficiently using human, fiscal, and technological resources in a school environment; promoting and protecting the welfare and safety of school students and staff; developing school capacity for distributed leadership; and ensuring that teacher and organizational time is focused to support high-quality instruction and student learning.

ABSTRACT

The changing demographics of a community often complicate school decisions because of stakeholders' expectations. Therefore, principals find themselves at the forefront of political systems that shape and reshape a school and the larger community. In this case, the principal is faced with just such a problem involving budget needs, curriculum revisions, personnel issues, and more. What can he do to keep everyone happy or at least happy enough for him to keep his job?

OBJECTIVES

1. The principal works collaboratively with stakeholders to develop campus plans.
2. The principal applies understanding of the larger political, social, economic, legal, and cultural context to develop activities and policies that benefit the school community.
3. The principal demonstrates the ability to communicate with diverse members of a school community concerning trends in the school environment.
4. The principal advocates for policies and programs that promote equitable learning opportunities and success for all students.

LITERATURE REVIEW

Organizational Power and Politics

The political arenas of organizations are composed of coalitions of individuals who attempt to determine how power is distributed (Cyert and March 1963). These interest groups represent a variety of associations, have both internal and external interests, and adhere to a diversity of values, beliefs, and perceptions. Typically, these differences are stable and slow to change and cause much tension and conflict, especially in the critical area of allocating scarce resources (Hoy and Miskel 2001).

Clegg, Kornberger, and Pitsis (2011) described organizations as structures that are built on formal and informal norms used to organize the actions of a diverse group of people. Ensuring that these people with varied backgrounds, interests, and understandings follow the norms means engaging in dialogue about power and ethics. The researchers defined power as a concept that incorporates the procedures, processes, and dispositions that attempt to ensure that people act according to the organization's rules. Ethics is described as doing the right things in the right way.

Hirschman (in Hoy and Miskel 2001) observed that participants in any organization have three basic options: leave, stay and try to change the system, and stay and contribute as expected. Those who choose to stay and try to change the system become players in the power game. These individuals, in order to be effective, must have the energy and the skill to act strategically when necessary.

Effective Leadership in the Political Arena

The ongoing attention on accountability often has school leaders feeling that dealing with politics is a separate role from educating children (Changing role 2007). Detrich (2001) suggested that "placing student learning at the heart of the enterprise is something that must be done within the arena of politics, not despite it" (23). According to the National Association of Secondary School Principals' report (Changing role 2007) an important role of the school leadership is to develop economic and political dialogue with all stakeholders regarding educating children. Whether they want to or not, school leaders must be active participants in the political arena of education. Their challenge is to equalize leadership and politics.

While politics is common to all organizations, its most common consequence based on the distribution of power is generally conflict. Political action can be both conflictive and cooperative (Blase 1991), and while there is no guarantee that those who become powerful will use it appropriately, power and politics are not always destructive and can be a means to achieve noble purposes (Bolman and Deal 1997). Being successful politically "requires organizational members to bargain, negotiate, jockey for position, and engage in a variety of political games, strategies and tactics to influence the goals and decisions of their organizations" (Hoy and Miskel 2001, 238).

Vecchio (1988) identified a set of political tactics commonly used at all levels:

- Ingratiating—gaining goodwill of another through doing favors or being attentive
- Networking—forming relationships with influential people
- Information management—obtaining important information, then using it skillfully to control others
- Impression management—creating a favorable image
- Coalition building—grouping together to achieve common objectives
- Scapegoating—blaming and attacking others

COMMUNITY INFLUENCE AND SCHOOL MICROPOLITICS

The micropolitical perspective on organizations provides a valuable approach to understanding day-to-day life in schools. Seminal author Iannaccone (1975) considered micropolitics in two ways: the interaction of administrators, teachers, and students within the school and interactions between lay and professional groups at the school building level. In other words, what happens inside schools cannot be completely understood without a knowledge of the environment in which schools operate. Micropolitics is concerned with power and how it is used to influence and protect oneself and others.

Blase (1991) explained micropolitics as being "about conflict and how people compete . . . to get what they want. It is about cooperation and how people build support . . . to achieve their ends. It is about what people in all social settings think about and have strong feelings about, what is so often unspoken and not easily observed" (1).

A critical power component of micropolitics is visibility (Corbett 1991) and its influence on certain norms. Leaders must model the behaviors and norms of the professional community, ensuring that the vision is alive and visible (Changing role 2007). For example, increased visibility of teachers' role performances to supervisors enables supervisors to reinforce common expectations of behavior, encourage innovations, and address deviations from the norm. Through increased visibility, expectations become so ingrained within the organization that new members quickly understand appropriate school practices.

Parents and other community members have potentially powerful influence when they have greater access to information than administrators do about what is happening in classes. The very visibility of a teacher's role is available to parents through their children's eyes, by parents hearing children talk about school, by parents seeing their children's schoolwork habits, when the community sees children's public behavior, and by parents talking with each other about what their children have heard or said about school.

Consequently, what happens within the school building during the school day is not isolated to the school environment alone but is instead connected to the larger community through the concept of visibility. This interconnectedness leads to a school's local community contributing to expectations that shape behavior of those who work in the school. In this way, the community represents a constant source of concern for local educators, and the principal, along with the superintendent, is usually the entry point (Corbett 1991). In other words, the principal's behavior can encourage (or discourage) community desires by influencing teachers.

Conflict Management

Because power and organizational politics inevitably create differing levels of conflict, effective principals spend a substantial amount of time and energy mediating circumstances where individual needs and expectations of the organization conflict. These leaders manage conflict by providing opportunities for risk-free discussion, emphasizing community values, and being willing to live with the uncertainty as the participants work through the conflict (Changing role 2007).

Thomas (in Hoy and Miskel 2001) identified two basic dimensions of behavior that produce conflict: attempting to satisfy organizational demands and attempting to meet the needs of individual members. The dimension of satisfying organizational needs is considered along an assertive-unassertive continuum, while the dimension attempting to satisfy individual member needs is considered from uncooperative to cooperative.

Thomas (1976; 1977) examined five styles of conflict management: avoiding, compromising, competing, accommodating, and collaborating. Each of the styles has a level of effectiveness when used in the appropriate situation. For example, an avoiding style on the continuum is unassertive and uncooperative. Here the principal ignores conflicts, and in the case of trivial issues or when things just need to "cool off," for example, this can be effective. Another example is that of accommodating, which is unassertive and cooperative on the continuum. In this style, the principal gives in to the demands of the subordinate, which would be an appropriate strategy to use, for example, when the principal discovers he has made a mistake or wants to build goodwill toward other more important issues (see Hoy and Miskel 2001, 245–47).

Harris and Jenkins (2013) argued that during much of the school day leaders are engaged in resolving conflicts that arise regarding curriculum, instruction, personnel, students, parents, discipline, budget, and community issues, as well as other school-related needs. Clearly, school conflict is rooted in understandings of the cultural issues on a campus. Quantz (2007) noted that schools are made up of "individuals and groups who need to find themselves in a place where their identities" are recognized and valued (55).

Therefore, leaders must understand the political nature of cultural conflicts in order to lead groups to resolution. Harris and Jenkins (2013) recommended a four-step Framework for Analyzing Cultural Conflict. The steps
are:

- Step 1 – Identify the nature of the cultural conflict
- Step 2 – Consider the choices and the possible consequences
- Step 3 – Implement appropriate conflict strategies
- Step 4 – Commit to continuing on or commit to moving forward in cultu-
  ral understandings.

Implementing Educational Policy

Hope (2002) defined policies as "politically derived interventions . . . whose
purpose is to resolve a perceived societal problem" (40). Because many
perceive that public schools are failing, legislators have mandated a variety
of policies intended to strengthen certification requirements, improve accountability, and increase student performance and curriculum standards, to
name just a few.

As evidenced in a 2013 National Science Teachers Association (NSTA)
legislative update on the reauthorization of the Elementary and Secondary
Education Act a 1,150-page plan was presented that would not only freeze
No Child Left Behind, Race to the Top, and the administration's use of
waivers, but would create more than twenty-five new programs as well as
more than 150 new reporting requirements for states and local school districts (NSTA 2013). Today's educators are continually faced with implementing new policies. Implementation is rarely an easy task because of a
variety of obstacles, such as lack of resources, insufficient time, disagree-
ment about how to achieve results, and sometimes the implementer's own
indifference to the specific policy.

Policies relating to mandates, such as inclusion, zero tolerance, school
safety, grouping, scheduling, dress code, technology, and budgeting, all require the principal as an advocate for successful implementation. Hope
(2002) suggests the following considerations for principals in implementing
policy:

- Embrace the educational policy; otherwise, being negative may reinforce
  staff resistance, while a positive attitude can influence how teachers respond to the policy and its training;

- Conceptualize the policy in the school context by creating a vision of the policy and its meaning for the school;
- Demystify the policy through information disclosure;
- Provide staff development for successful policy implementation;
- Provide encouragement for policy implementation;
- Monitor and evaluate policy implementation;

CASE STUDY

The Attaway Consolidated School District had experienced significant growth in recent years as the small town of Attaway changed from a rural agricultural village to a bedroom community. As new subdivisions were built, families moved from the nearby state capital to Attaway. The student population of the Attaway Consolidated School District has more than doubled in the past ten years. Voters recently approved a bond issue that would provide funding for construction of two new elementary campuses, a middle school, and a high school.

Attaway High School was literally bursting at the seams with more than twenty-five hundred students crowded into a facility designed for a capacity of one thousand. Recent curriculum revision and alignment projects resulted in adoption of a new master schedule with the addition of new courses, such as more computer courses, Advanced Placement courses, and a concurrent credit program with Culberson County Community College.

Because of decreased student enrollment, woodworking and other shop courses were being phased out. There has been discussion about modifying the existing agriculture program to include canine and equine science, wildlife management, and nontechnical offerings, such as floral design and landscaping; however, veteran agriculture teacher Calvin Simon has opposed these changes, and they were never made.

Calvin had provided leadership for thirty years for a very successful agriculture program. His expertise in animal husbandry and livestock judging programs had been instrumental in a number of state championships for Attaway High School agriculture students at state competitions. One of his former students, James Stephens, was now Attaway Consolidated School District's assistant superintendent for administration.

Although student interest in the agriculture program, as evidenced by enrollment in the elective courses, had dwindled considerably in recent years, Calvin continued to receive a sizable portion of the school's discretionary

budget. Last year, campus-level budget committee meetings had been especially stressful when Calvin had vigorously lobbied for members to fund
several agriculture projects that other committee members had questioned.

Yesterday, Calvin and Terry Jackson, the other agriculture teacher, met
with Attaway High School principal Dan Lewis to request support for a new
plan to increase the agriculture program through a cooperative arrangement
with one of the local wealthy landowners. The proposed program, which
would encourage students to buy cattle or sheep for livestock projects that
could be housed at a local farm, would require a sizable increase in the
agriculture program's budget for next year. "How can you expect us to build
a program if you continually cut our budget?" had been Calvin's mantra
during yesterday's conference. "You're just trying to kill the agriculture
program."

The idea for reviving the animal husbandry program had been presented
at a time when enrollment in the agriculture program warranted only one
teacher, not the two currently assigned. Terry Jackson had spoken to the
principal just this morning in private and reminded him that "if you need to
cut back a teacher, I'm certified to teach biology."

As if this was not enough, just yesterday the principal had run into the
high school's PTA president at the grocery store where she had "cornered"
him for ten minutes about the need to broaden Advanced Placement offerings. She had also told him that she and several interested parents would be
making an appointment with him sometime this week to discuss some ideas
they had.

Demands for the discretionary funding were greater than ever. Urgent
needs included new computers, graphing calculators for the math classes,
band instruments, and a myriad of other instructional needs. There was also
growing conflict within the community. While the older community members still talked with pride about the agriculture program, the newer residents, who were generally younger and more affluent, were more concerned
with the high school college preparatory program.

What should the principal do?

DISCUSSION QUESTIONS

1. Identify areas of conflict facing this principal.
2. How would you prioritize them?

3. What policies guide the use of discretionary budget items at your school? Use your policies in solving this aspect of the problem.

4. In what ways could a site-based management council help or hurt in this situation?

5. Consider the conflict management styles discussed in the literature review. Frame each of the five styles within the areas of conflict you identified in question 1. What might the possible effects be?

6. What are the cultural conflicts inherent in this case?

7. Create a visual to show the micropolitical factors within this case.

8. Reflect on how political your actions are in leading your school.

9. What policies would you suggest that the school in the case adopt to reduce some of the conflicts?

10. Interview individuals who have served on a site-based committee at their school. How political did they find the experience? In what ways? Ask them to describe specific situations.

11. How do you feel effective principals should use power?

ON YOUR OWN—CONSIDER

You have both Advanced Placement (AP) and dual enrollment courses at your high school. AP courses are weighted and dual enrollment courses are not. Of the 120 AP English students, fewer than 5 percent pass the AP exams and receive college credit. Of the seventy-five students enrolled in dual enrollment, 100 percent make an A or B and receive college credit. Parents of the students enrolled in dual enrollment courses have requested that the district approve weighted grades for those courses. Their complaint is that the dual enrollment courses are more rigorous than the AP courses and that the policy of weighted grades is not equitable.

You and your assistant principal conduct walk-through visits in the English AP and dual enrollment classrooms for a six-week period. After meeting with your assistant principal and comparing data, you conclude that the curriculum is more rigorous in the dual enrollment classroom. You make a recommendation to the board to weight the grades for the dual enrollment courses. After much discussion, the board does not approve the recommendation. You know that the reason is because the board president's sister teaches the AP courses for which she received a stipend. If the students in the dual enrollment receive weighted grades, she is afraid her program will suffer. What are your next steps?

REMEMBER

The principal knows how to apply principles of effective leadership and management in relation to campus budgeting, personnel, resource utilization, financial management, and technology use.

REFERENCES

Blase, J. 1991. Micropolitical perspective. In The politics of life in schools: Power, conflict, and cooperation (1–17). Newbury Park, CA: Sage.

Bolman, L. G., and T. E. Deal. 1997. Reframing organizations: Artistry, choice, and leadership. 2nd ed. San Francisco: Jossey-Bass.

Changing role of the middle level and high school leader: Learning from the past preparing for the future. 2007. Retrieved from National Association of Secondary School Principals, www.nassp.org/changingrole.

Clegg, S., Kornberger, M., and Pitsis, T. (2011). Managing and organizations: An introduction to theory and practice. 3rd ed. Thousand Oaks, CA: Sage.

Corbett, H. D. 1991. Community influence and school micropolitics. In The politics of life in schools: Power, conflict, and cooperation (73–95). Edited by J. Blase. Newbury Park, CA: Sage.

Cyert, R., and J. March. 1963. A behavioral theory of the firm. Englewood Cliffs, NJ: Prentice Hall.

Detrich, R. (2001). Is politics in education here to stay? Viewpoints. Naperville, IL: North Central Regional Educational Laboratory. Retrieved from www.ncrel.org/policy/pubs/html/viewpt/index.html.

Harris, S., and S. Jenkins. 2013. Conflicts in culture. Lanham, MD: Rowman & Littlefield Publishers.

Hope, W. 2002. Implementing educational policy: Some considerations for principals. Clearing House 76, no. 1: 40–43.

Hoy, W., and C. Miskel. 2001. Educational administration: Theory, research, and practice. 6th ed. Boston: McGraw-Hill.

Iannaccone, L. 1975. Education policy systems: A study guide for educational administrators. Fort Lauderdale, FL: Nova University.

National Science Teachers Association (NSTA) legislative update. 2013, June 17. Retrieved from science.nsta.org/nstaexpress/nstaexpress_2013_06_17_legupdate.htm.

Thomas, K. 1976. Conflict and conflict management. In Handbook of industrial and organizational psychology (889 –936). Edited by M. D. Dunnette. Chicago: Rand McNally.

———. 1977. Toward multi-dimensional values in teaching: The example of conflict behaviors. Academy of Management Review 20: 486–90.

Vecchio, R. P. 1988. Organizational behavior. Chicago: Dryden.

ADDITIONAL RESOURCES

Fowler, F. 2000. Policy studies for educational leaders. Upper Saddle River, NJ: Prentice Hall.

Matthews, L., and G. Crow. 2003. Principal as politician. In Being and becoming a principal (197–223). Boston: Allyn & Bacon.

Reagan, T. G., C. W. Case, and J. W. Brubacher. 2000. Becoming a reflective educator: How to build a culture on inquiry in the schools. Thousand Oaks, CA: Corwin Press.

Chapter Nine

We're Scared Every Day

Texas Standard Competency 009: The principal knows how to apply principles of leadership and management to the campus physical plant and support systems to ensure a safe and effective learning environment.

TACS Standard 3 (2014): Executive Leadership. The principal is responsible for modeling a consistent focus on and commitment to improving student learning.

ELCC Standard 3.0 (2011): A building-level education leader applies knowledge that promotes the success of every student by ensuring the management of the school organization, operation, and resources through monitoring and evaluating the school management and operational systems; efficiently using human, fiscal, and technological resources in a school environment; promoting and protecting the welfare and safety of school students and staff; developing school capacity for distributed leadership; and ensuring that teacher and organizational time is focused to support high-quality instruction and student learning.

ABSTRACT

The case study that follows focuses on creating schools that are safe places for faculty and for the students. The school must consider policies for safety and how to implement them in such a way that student learning is optimum. Another issue to be considered is that of communicating with the public so that it has confidence that community schools provide safe environments for children.

OBJECTIVES

The principal develops plans of action for focusing on effective organization and management of fiscal, human, and material resources, giving priority to student learning, safety, curriculum, and instruction.

1. The principal develops communications plans for staff that includes opportunities for staff to develop their family and community collaboration skills.
2. The principal demonstrates an understanding of how to apply legal principles to promote educational equity and provide safe, effective, and efficient facilities.
3. The principal develops and implements procedures for crisis planning and for responding to crises.

LITERATURE REVIEW

Schools face daily threats of violence. In the school year 2009–2010, 85 percent of public schools reported the occurrence of some type of criminal incident resulting in approximately 1.9 million school-based crimes (Robers, Zhang, and Truman 2012). From July 1, 2009, to June 30, 2010, there were thirty-three school-associated violent deaths; of these, twenty-five were homicides and five were suicides. During that same time period, 23 percent of schools reported incidents of bullying among students on a weekly or daily basis while 16 percent of public schools reported the occurrence of gang activity. In the same year, approximately 74 percent of schools reported at least one violent incident, 44 percent reported one or more thefts, 46 percent reported at least one act of vandalism, and 16 percent reported a serious violent crime (Snyder and Dillow 2012). From July 1, 2010, through November 14, 2013, there were seventy-four school-associated violent deaths in elementary and secondary schools in the United States (Robers, Kemp, Rathbun, and Morgan 2014).

According to Hinduja and Patchin (2014), another safety challenge facing schools today is cyber-bullying which has become a growing problem due to the numbers of kids are who have embraced social networking. Kids have been bullying each other for generations; however, technology has allowed them to expand their reach and the extent of their harm. Cyber-bullying is defined as "willful and repeated harm inflicted through the use of computers, cell phones, and other electronic devices" (1). This is where technology is used to harass, threaten, and humiliate others. In 2011, 37 percent of sixth graders reported being bullied at school, compared with 30 percent of seventh graders, 31 percent of eighth graders, 26 percent of ninth graders, 28 percent of tenth graders, 24 percent of eleventh graders, and 22 percent of twelfth graders.

Thus, considering statistics, security in America's schools must continue to be a major concern. Teachers cannot teach effectively in an atmosphere of violence, and students cannot learn when the school climate is one of fear for personal safety. "Media, video games, and music all tell kids that the way to solve interpersonal problems is through violence. In the 1970s, kids used to fight with their fists; now, when kids have arguments, one of them goes home and gets his Uzi," said Kevin Dwyer, the president of the National Association for School Psychologists (Dwyer, Osher, and Wagner 1998).

Research studies have suggested when violence is part of a child's life. It negatively affects that child's learning ability (Massey 2000; Prothrow-Stith and Quaday 1995). Yet while the American Psychological Association (2000) does not blame schools, it does indicate that there are several components of a school organization that create a climate that leads to aggression, such as overcrowding and imposing overly restrictive behavioral routines. In addition, adolescence is often characterized by higher rates of violence than other stages of life. Youth living in communities with high levels of observed violent behaviors are more likely to be victims of violence and engage in violent behaviors (Center for the Study and Prevention of Violence 2009). The presence of gangs in the vicinity of schools can contribute to the presence of fear and increase aggressive behavior (Forber-Pratt, Aragon, and Espelage 2013).

Descriptors of a Safe School

Schools can do much to prevent violence when a safe and responsive climate is in place. The creation of an emergency plan is vital to preparing school stakeholders for possible crises. Crisis planning includes the phases of prevention/mitigation, preparedness, response, and recovery (U.S. Department of Education 2008). Planning is a necessary step in preparing school campuses for potential crisis scenarios. School safety cannot be accomplished by one person or program. Rather, it should be framed within effective comprehensive and collaborative efforts that require and utilize dedicated, committed school staff and relevant community stakeholders (Cowan and Payne 2013).

For example, safe schools support learning and socially appropriate behaviors. This can be done by focusing strongly on creating a support base for academics and helping students achieve high standards. Safe schools encourage students and staff to develop positive relationships within the school and within the community. In addition, safe schools understand that safety and order are necessary for children to develop appropriate social, emotional, and academic skills. Dwyer, Osher, and Warger (1998) identified a set of descriptors for school communities where safe schools are being responsive to the needs of children. These descriptors include the following:

- Focusing on academic achievement for all students while allowing for individual differences
- Involving families in meaningful ways and making parents feel welcome
- Developing links to the community to enhance the use of resources
- Supporting children in developing positive relationships with faculty and with one another
- Discussing safety issues by teaching about the dangers of firearms and teaching strategies for dealing with anger and conflicts
- Treating students with equal respect
- Creating ways for students to safely report concerns about potentially dangerous situations
- Having a system for referring children who are suspected victims of neglect or abuse
- Offering programs for children before and after school
- Promoting good citizenship and character development

Verdugo and Schneider (1999) studied the characteristics of quality schools and the characteristics of safe schools and found that quality schools hold five broad traits in common: (a) a shared commitment to high student achievement; (b) open communication and collaboration; (c) continuous assessment for learning and teaching; (d) personal and professional learning; and (e) availability of resources to support teaching and learning. They found important relationships between school quality, safe-school components, and the seriousness of school violence. Quality schools are less likely to be characterized by serious crime or violence, and quality schools are more likely to have safe-school components in place. This suggests that while it is important to work toward making schools safe, schools that work to develop quality schools will be developing safe schools.

Appropriate Support for Zero-Tolerance Policies

Too often in the past, teachers have been left to deal with potentially violent situations in whatever way they chose. Boards of education have often reacted impulsively and imposed plans that were simplistic and heavily authoritarian. This has been observed in some zero-tolerance policies that have mandated predetermined consequences for specific offenses regardless of the circumstances or disciplinary history of the student involved. Occasionally, this blanket enforcement of discipline policies has backfired. For example, a six-year-old with a plastic knife placed in his lunch box by his grandmother was disciplined. A middle school girl who shared her asthma inhaler on the school bus with a friend having a wheezing attack was suspended for drug trafficking (Tebo 2000).

While zero-tolerance policies have been effective in some areas of the country, these policies must be implemented with discernment (Underwood, Lewis, Pickett, and Worona 2000). Therefore, a well-thought-out discipline plan, collaboratively developed with input from teachers as well as students and parents, can help keep such arbitrary rules from contributing to violence.

Texas has devised an innovative approach to zero tolerance that sets out three levels of violations. At the most serious level are offenses such as bringing a gun or long-bladed knife to school, which merits expulsion and the requirement to attend a county alternative school. The next level are offenses such as misdemeanor drug possession and simple assault, which result in temporarily removal of students from school and placement in an alternative education setting within their own school district. The lowest level of offense includes inappropriate actions, such as acting out within the classroom, where school officials have discretion to determine the consequences (Tebo 2000).

Dealing with Crisis Situations

"The best defense against random violence is a comprehensive school security plan that is as concerned with routine fist fights among students as it is with the attack by an armed intruder" (Baldwin 1999, 11). According to Brown, Saunders, Harris, and Castile (2013) the creation of an emergency plan is critical to preparing school leaders for possible crises. Crisis planning

includes four basic components: prevention/mitigation, preparedness, response, and recovery. Each of these steps involves school leaders working
with law enforcement and mental health agencies.

- Prevention/mitigation—the focus of prevention or mitigation is to decrease the incidence of violent episodes and to reduce the impacts of
  disasters. Strategies to do this include conducting audits of the school
  climate, identifying and determining the violence prevention needs of the
  school, and working with local emergency managers and first responders.
- Preparedness—Preparedness actions engage support and require the involvement of all stakeholders in planning, identifying, and acquiring necessary equipment and supplies. Communication procedures must be developed also. Strategies to do this include establishing an assessment
  team, conducting needs, hazards, and treat assessments, and developing
  action plans.
- Response—A necessary component of any crisis plan is to have a separate
  response plan. Components of this response plan must include establishing close communication with first responders, standardizing training, and
  acknowledging a chain of command. Strategies that must be in place for
  emergency actions include lockdowns, lockouts, shelter-in-place, evacua-
  tion and release and reunification.
- Recovery—Recovery is the process of restoring the school to a learning
  environment as quickly as possible. Recovery strategies include providing
  time for recovery progress, providing time to support students and school
  personnel, and identifying things that can be incorporated into future planning.

Informing the Media

In the past few years, nearly every school district in America has developed a
specific plan for dealing with the media. Along with adoption of this plan,
staff development should be provided to be assured of appropriate implementation should a crisis occur. It is recommended that a single spokesperson be
designated for the school to collect, coordinate, and release information to
the media (Baldwin 1999). The following are some suggested guidelines for
handling the media:

- Do not panic
- Develop a written statement concerning the crisis (when this is possible)

- Contact the press before they contact you
- Develop media-on-campus guidelines and restrictions
- Never refuse to speak to the media
- Do not overreact or exaggerate any situation
- Give only factual and verified informational statements
- Do not try to avoid blame by using a scapegoat
- Stress positive action taken by the school district
- Do not talk off the record
- Do not argue with media personnel (Decker 1997, 56)

When informing the media, school personnel must remember that it is imperative to keep a positive attitude; no matter what the crisis, every attempt must be made for calmness to prevail.

CASE STUDY

Smithton High School is a large high school in a middle-income suburban community. During the past month, there have been several disturbing discipline incidents at the school reported in the *Smithton Daily Reporter*. This has caused a great deal of discussion about safety issues at Smithton High School and the other twelve Smithton Integrated School District (ISD) campuses.

Just last night, Smithton ISD superintendent Donald Hawkins discussed safety and student discipline in a television interview. He strongly contended that Smithton High School was a safe and effective learning environment and that misconduct would not be tolerated. In fact, he said, "The Smithton High School principal and faculty are committed to taking the appropriate disciplinary measures to remove students from campus who disrupt the learning process." Then he even said that the "media is just blowing everything out of proportion."

What happened at the high school? A shoving match between two students escalated into a fight, with the fighters encouraged by a crowd of students. When assistant principal Bryant McGarrity attempted to break up the fight and escort the fighters to the office, several of the onlookers pushed him to the ground and kicked him. Although he was not seriously injured, the incident was totally unacceptable, and the offending students were reassigned to the Sherlock County Alternative School, as mandated by the Smithton High School Code of Student Conduct.

Two days after the fight, a ninth-grade honor student was assaulted and robbed by two students in the bus loading area after school. The teachers on duty at the bus loading area did not witness the incident, and the three students who attacked the ninth grader were gone by the time teachers arrived. Other students had witnessed the assault but did not intervene or try to help the student who was being assaulted. The injured student was transported to Smithton Regional Hospital, where he was kept overnight with a concussion and injuries to his eye. The school was still in the process of investigating the incident.

A few days later, four girls accosted two female students as they walked home from school. Although they were not injured, their purses and book bags were stolen, and they were threatened with harm if they told authorities. The city police department investigated the incident and Smithton chief of police Jack Perry was quoted in the *Smithton Daily Reporter*, "If the school people can't control things, we will."

Then yesterday there was a bomb threat at the high school. The alert came to the attention of school officials at 9:00 a.m. when a message warning about the bomb threat was found on the wall of a boys' bathroom. Students were immediately sent home while school police and other school personnel searched school lockers, classrooms, and other places at the school where a bomb could have been planted. School resumed almost four hours later.

This morning, Smithton High School principal Thomas Newton was dismayed to learn that a group of parents had written a letter to the editor of the *Smithton Daily Reporter* relating that Smithton High School was a dangerous place to work, that student discipline was a joke, and that students and teachers were "afraid every day!"

DISCUSSION QUESTIONS

1. What is the first step you would take as principal of Smithton High School to resolve this situation?
2. In what ways would you involve the community in this situation?
3. Create an organizational action plan for the principal to submit to the superintendent that would lead to resolution of the problems at Smithton High School.
4. Write a crisis management plan for this school. Who would you involve in this process?

5. Contact area schools or your own school and bring a copy of your crisis management plan to class.

6. What strategies would you implement to involve the media in a positive way in reporting about Smithton High School?

7. Locate a policy book from ten years ago or interview a principal who has been at the same school for at least ten years and compare and contrast safety procedures that were in place then and now.

8. Divide into groups and role-play an interview between the designated speaker to the media and a television reporter regarding the events in the case study.

9. What community resources would you involve in the resolution of this case?

10. How would zero-tolerance policies contribute to this case?

ON YOUR OWN—CONSIDER

Sara is a seventh grader at your school. She has been in and out of foster care since she was six months old. As a result, she has attended nine schools. Making friends has been very difficult and so she began using video chat in the seventh grade to meet new people online. One stranger convinced the teenager to take inappropriate pictures and to post them on a Facebook page he had set up. The picture began circulating on the Internet, including a Facebook profile that used the photograph as the profile image. In addition, Sara was being harassed and blackmailed through text messaging and social media. She began skipping school and her grades suffered. You uncover information that a group of eighth-grade girls are behind the cyber-bullying of Sara. What do you do as the principal?

REFERENCES

American Psychological Association. 2000. Warning signs. Washington, DC: Author. Brochure.

Baldwin, H. 1999. Planning for disaster: A guide for school administrators. Bloomington, IN: Phi Delta Kappa Educational Foundation.

Brown, C., T. Saunders, S. Harris, and H. Castile. 2013. NCPEA Policy Brief: School safety: Implications for policy and practice 2, no. 1. Retrieved from www.ncpeapublications.org.

Center for the Study and Prevention of Violence. 2009. Ethnicity, race, class and adolescent violence (CSPV Fact Sheet FS-003). Boulder, CO: University of Colorado.

Cowan, K., and C. Paine. 2013. School safety: What really works. Principal Leadership 13, no. 7: 12–16.

Decker, R. 1997. When a crisis hits will your school be ready? Thousand Oaks, CA: Corwin Press.

Dwyer, K., D. Osher, and C. Warger. 1998. Early warning, timely response: A guide to safe schools. Washington, DC: U.S. Department of Education.

Forber-Pratt, A. J., Aragon, S. R., and Espelage, D. L. 2013. The influence of gang presence on victimization in one middle school environment. Psychology of Violence, Advance online publication. doi: 10.1037/a0031835.

Harris, S., and Jenkins, S. 2013. Conflicts in culture: Strategies to understand and resolve issues. Lanham, MD: Rowman & Littlefield.

Hinduja, S., and Patchin, J. W. 2014. Cyberbullying Identification, Prevention, and Response. Cyberbullying Research Center. Retrieved from www.cyberbullying.us.

Massey, M. 2000. The effects of violence on young children. The ERIC Review: School safety: A collaborative effort 7, no. 1. Retrieved from www.accesseric.org/re-sources/ericreview/vol7no1/effects.html.

Prothrow-Stith, D., and S. Quaday. 1995. Hidden casualties: The relationship between violence and learning. Washington, DC: National Health and Education Consortium and National Consortium for African-American Children. ERIC Document Reproduction Service No. ED 390 552.

Quantz, R. A. 2007. Rethinking systems and conflict in schools. In D. Carlson and C. P. Gause (eds), Keeping the promise: Essays on leadership, democracy, and education (46–60). New York: Peter Lang.

Robers, S., J. Kemp, A. Rathbun, and R. Morgan. 2014. Indicators of school crime and safety: 2013. National Center for Education Statistics, U.S. Department of Education, and Bureau of Justice Statistics, Office of Justice Programs, U.S. Department of Justice. Retrieved from: nces.ed.gov or bjs.ojp.usdoj.gov.

Robers, S., J. Zhang, and J. Truman. 2012. Indicators of school crime and safety: 2011 (NCES 2012-002/NCJ 236021). Washington, DC: National Center for Education Statistics, U.S. Department of Education, and Bureau of Justice Statistics, Office of Justice Programs, U.S. Department of Justice. Retrieved from www.bjs.gov/content/pub/pdf/iscs11.pdf.

Snyder, T. D., and S. A. Dillow. 2012. Digest of education statistics 2011 (NCES 2012-001). Washington, DC: National Center for Education Statistics, Institute of Education Sciences, U.S. Department of Education. Retrieved from nces.ed.gov/pubs2012/2012001.pdf.

Tebo, M. 2000. Zero tolerance, zero sense. ABA Journal 86: 40–47.

Underwood, J., J. Lewis, D. Pickett, and J. Worona. 2000. School safety: Working together to keep schools safe. Retrieved from www.keepschoolssafe.org/school.html [accessed April 11, 2000].

U.S. Department of Education, Office of Safe and Drug-Free Schools. 2008. A guide to school vulnerability assessments: Key principles for safe schools. Washington, DC: Author. Retrieved from rems.ed.gov/docs/VA_Report_2008.pdf.

Verdugo, R., and J. Schneider. 1999. Quality schools, safe schools: A theoretical and empirical discussion. Education & Urban Society 31, no. 3: 286–308.

ADDITIONAL RESOURCES

Bosworth, K., L. Ford, and D. Hernandez. 2011. School climate factors contributing to student and faculty perceptions of safety and select Arizona schools. Journal of School Health 81, no.4: 194–201.

Coordinating Council on Juvenile Justice and Delinquency Prevention. 1996. Combating violence and delinquency: The National Juvenile Justice Action Plan. Washington, DC: Coordinating Council on Juvenile Justice and Delinquency Prevention.

DiGiulio, R. C. 2001. Educate, medicate, or litigate? What teachers, parents, and administrators must do about student behavior. Thousand Oaks, CA: Corwin Press.

Duke, D. 2002. Creating safe schools for all children. Boston: Allyn & Bacon.

Friedland, S. 1999. Violence reduction: Start with school culture. School Administrator 56, no. 5: 14–16.

Harris, S., and J. Harris. 2000. Youth violence and suggestions for schools to reduce the violence. Journal of At-Risk Issues 7, no. 2: 21–27.

Lewis, A. 1999. Listen to the children. Phi Delta Kappan 80, no. 10: 723–24.

Lunenburg, F. C., and A. Ornstein. 2000. Educational administration: Concepts and practices. 3rd ed. Belmont, CA: Wadsworth/Thomson Learning.

Sanders, J. R. 2000. Evaluating school programs. 2nd ed. Thousand Oaks, CA: Corwin Press.

Williams, W. 1998. Preventing violence in school: What can principals do? NASSP Bulletin 82, no. 603: 10–17.

ADDITIONAL ELECTRONIC RESOURCES

Federal Government

Federal Bureau of Investigation (FBI):

- Law Enforcement Bulletin: Addressing School Violence: www.fbi.gov/statsservices/publications/law-enforcement-bulletin/may_2011/school_violence.

U.S. Department of Education:

- Indicators of School Crime and Safety 2011: nces.ed.gov/pubs2012/2012002rev.pdf.
- Office of Safe and Healthy Students: www2.ed.gov/about/offices/list/oese/oshs/index.html.

U.S. Department of Homeland Security:

- School Safety: www.dhs.gov/school-safety.
- Federal Emergency Management Agency (FEMA):

  - Ready.gov: www.ready.gov/kids.
  - Building a Disaster-Resistant University: www.fema.gov/hazard-mitigation-assistance/building-disaster-resistant-university.
  - National Preparedness Directorate: training.fema.gov/.

U.S. Secret Service:

- Threat Assessment in Schools: A Guide to Managing Threatening Situations and to Creating Safe School Climates: www.secretservice.gov/ntac/ssi_guide.pdf.
- National Threat Assessment Center Secret Service Safe School Initiative: www.secretservice.gov/ntac_ssi.shtml.

State Government: Texas School Safety Center: txssc.txstate.edu/.

Nongovernmental Organizations: Stop Bullying Now: stopbullyingnow.com/index.htm#.

Center for the Study and Prevention of Violence, University of Colorado at Boulder: www.colorado.edu/cspv.

Appendix 1

ELCC Standards for Advanced Programs in Educational Leadership for Principals

School Building Leadership

ELCC Standards for Advanced Programs in Educational Leadership for Principals—School Building Leadership

National Policy Board for Educational Administration, published November, 2011

Source: ncate.org

ELCC STANDARD 1.0

A building-level education leader applies knowledge that promotes the success of every student by collaboratively facilitating the development, articulation, implementation, and stewardship of a shared school vision of learning through the collection and use of data to identify school goals, assess organizational effectiveness, and implement school plans to achieve school goals; promotion of continual and sustainable school improvement; and evaluation of school progress and revision of school plans supported by school-based stakeholders.

ELCC Standard Elements

ELCC 1.1: Candidates understand and can collaboratively develop, articulate, implement, and steward a shared vision of learning for a school.

ELCC 1.2: Candidates understand and can collect and use data to identify school goals, assess organizational effectiveness, and implement plans to achieve school goals.

ELCC 1.3: Candidates understand and can promote continual and sustainable school improvement.

ELCC 1.4: Candidates understand and can evaluate school progress and revise school plans supported by school stakeholders.

ELCC STANDARD 2.0

A building-level education leader applies knowledge that promotes the success of every student by sustaining a school culture and instructional program conducive to student learning through collaboration, trust, and a personalized learning environment with high expectations for students; creating and evaluating a comprehensive, rigorous, and coherent curricular and instructional school program; developing and supervising the instructional and leadership capacity of school staff; and promoting the most effective and appropriate technologies to support teaching and learning within a school environment.

ELCC Standard Elements

ELCC 2.1: Candidates understand and can sustain a school culture and instructional program conducive to student learning through collaboration, trust, and a personalized learning environment with high expectations for students.

ELCC 2.2: Candidates understand and can create and evaluate a comprehensive, rigorous, and coherent curricular and instructional school program.

ELCC 2.3: Candidates understand and can develop and supervise the instructional and leadership capacity of school staff.

ELCC 2.4: Candidates understand and can promote the most effective and appropriate technologies to support teaching and learing in a school-level environment.

ELCC STANDARD 3.0

A building-level education leader applies knowledge that promotes the success of every student by ensuring the management of the school organization, operation, and resources through monitoring and evaluating the school management and operational systems; efficiently using human, fiscal, and technological resources in a school environment; promoting and protecting the welfare and safety of school students and staff; developing school capacity for distributed leadership; and ensuring that teacher and organizational time is focused to support high-quality instruction and student learning.

ELCC Standard Elements

ELCC 3.1: Candidates understand and can monitor and evaluate school management and operational systems.

ELCC 3.2: Candidates understand and can efficiently use human, fiscal, and technological resources to manage school operations.

ELCC 3.3: Candidates understand and can promote school-based policies and procedures that protect the welfare and safety of students and staff within the school.

ELCC 3.4: Candidates understand and can develop school capacity for distributed leadership.

ELCC 3.5: Candidates understand and can ensure teacher and organizational time focuses on supporting high-quality school instruction and student learning.

ELCC STANDARD 4.0

A building-level education leader applies knowledge that promotes the success of every student by collaborating with faculty and community members, responding to diverse community interests and needs, and mobilizing community resources on behalf of the school by collecting and analyzing information pertinent to improvement of the school's educational environment; promoting an understanding, appreciation, and use of the diverse cultural, social, and intellectual resources within the school community; building and sustaining positive school relationships with families and caregivers; and cultivating productive school relationships with community partners.

ELCC Standard Elements

ELCC 4.1: Candidates understand and can collaborate with faculty and community members by collecting and analyzing information pertinent to the improvement of the school's educational environment.

ELCC 4.2: Candidates understand and can mobilize community resources by promoting an understanding, appreciation, and use of diverse cultural, social, and intellectual resources within the school community.

ELCC 4.3: Candidates understand and can respond to community interests and needs by building and sustaining positive school relationships with families and caregivers.

ELCC 4.4: Candidates understand and can respond to community interests and needs by building and sustaining productive school relationships with community partners.

ELCC STANDARD 5.0

A building-level education leader applies knowledge that promotes the success of every student by acting with integrity, fairness, and in an ethical manner to ensure a school system of accountability for every student's academic and social success by modeling school principles of self-awareness, reflective practice, transparency, and ethical behavior as related to their roles within the school; safeguarding the values of democracy, equity, and diversity within the school; evaluating the potential moral and legal consequences of decision making in the school; and promoting social justice within the school to ensure that individual student needs inform all aspects of schooling.

ELCC Standard Elements

ELCC 5.1: Candidates understand and can act with integrity and fairness to ensure a school system of accountability for every student's academic and social success.

ELCC 5.2: Candidates understand and can model principles of self-awareness, reflective practice, transparency, and ethical behavior as related to their roles within the school.

ELCC 5.3: Candidates understand and can safeguard the values of democracy, equity, and diversity within the school.

ELCC 5.4: Candidates understand and can evaluate the potential moral and legal consequences of decision making in the school.

ELCC 5.5: Candidates understand and can promote social justice within the school to ensure that individual student needs inform all aspects of schooling.

ELCC STANDARD 6.0

A building-level education leader applies knowledge that promotes the success of every student by understanding, responding to, and influencing the larger political, social, economic, legal, and cultural context through advocating for school students, families, and caregivers; acting to influence local, district, state, and national decisions affecting student learning in a school environment; and anticipating and assessing emerging trends and initiatives in order to adapt school-based leadership strategies.

ELCC Standard Elements

ELCC 6.1: Candidates understand and can advocate for school students, families, and caregivers.

ELCC 6.2: Candidates understand and can act to influence local, district, state, and national decisions affecting student learning in a school environment.

ELCC 6.3: Candidates understand and can anticipate and assess emerging trends and initiatives in order to adapt school-based leadership strategies.

ELCC STANDARD 7.0

A building-level education leader applies knowledge that promotes the success of every student through a substantial and sustained educational leadership internship experience that has school-based field experiences and clinical internship practice within a school setting and is monitored by a qualified, on-site mentor.

ELCC Standard Elements

ELCC 7.1: Substantial Field and Clinical Internship Experience: The program provides significant field experiences and clinical internship practice for candidates within a school environment to synthesize and apply the content knowledge and develop professional skills identified in the other Educational Leadership Building-Level Program Standards through authentic, school-based leadership experiences.

ELCC 7.2: Sustained Internship Experience: Candidates are provided a six-month, concentrated (9–12 hours per week) internship that includes field experiences within a school-based environment.

ELCC 7.3: Qualified On-Site Mentor: An on-site school mentor who has demonstrated experience as an educational leader within a school and is selected collaboratively by the intern and program faculty with training by the supervising institution.

Appendix 2

Chapter 149. Commissioner's Rules Concerning Educator Standards Subchapter BB. Administrator Standards

Chapter 149. Commissioner's Rules Concerning Educator Standards Subchapter BB. Administrator Standards

(Adopted August 2014)

Source: www.tea.state.tx.us/index4.aspx?id=25769811630.

149.2001. PRINCIPAL STANDARDS

(a) Purpose. The standards, indicators, knowledge, and skills identified in this section shall be used to align with the training, appraisal, and professional development of principals.

(b) Standards.

(1) Standard 1—Instructional Leadership. The principal is responsible for ensuring every student receives high-quality instruction.

(A) Knowledge and skills.

(i) Effective instructional leaders:

(I) prioritize instruction and student achievement by developing and sharing a clear definition of high-quality instruction based on best practices from research;

(II) implement a rigorous curriculum aligned with state standards;

(III) analyze the curriculum to ensure that teachers align content across grades and that curricular scopes and sequences meet the particular needs of their diverse student populations;

(IV) model instructional strategies and set expectations for the content, rigor, and structure of lessons and unit plans; and

(V) routinely monitor and improve instruction by visiting classrooms, giving formative feedback to teachers, and attending grade or team meetings.

(ii) In schools led by effective instructional leaders, data are used to determine instructional decisions and monitor progress. Principals implement common interim assessment cycles to track classroom trends and determine appropriate interventions. Staff have the capacity to use data to drive effective instructional practices and interventions. The principal's focus on instruction results in a school filled with effective teachers who can describe, plan, and implement strong instruction, and classrooms filled with students actively engaged in cognitively challenging and differentiated activities.

(B) Indicators.

(i) Rigorous and aligned curriculum and assessment. The principal implements rigorous curricula and assessments aligned with state standards, including college and career readiness standards.

(ii) Effective instructional practices. The principal develops high-quality instructional practices among teachers that improve student learning.

(iii) Data-driven instruction and interventions. The principal monitors multiple forms of student data to inform instructional and intervention decisions and to close the achievement gap.

(2) Standard 2—Human Capital. The principal is responsible for ensuring there are high-quality teachers and staff in every classroom and throughout the school.

(A) Knowledge and skills.

(i) Effective leaders of human capital:

      (I) treat faculty/staff members as their most valuable resource and invest in the development, support, and supervision of the staff;

      (II) ensure all staff have clear goals and expectations that guide them and by which they are assessed;

      (III) are strategic in selecting and hiring candidates whose vision aligns with the school's vision and whose skills match the school's needs;

      (IV) ensure that, once hired, teachers develop and grow by building layered supports that include regular observations, actionable feedback, and coaching and school-wide supports so that teachers know how they are performing;

      (V) facilitate professional learning communities to review data and support development;

      (VI) create opportunities for effective teachers and staff to take on a variety of leadership roles and delegate responsibilities to staff and administrators on the leadership team; and

      (VII) use data from multiple points of the year to complete accurate evaluations of all staff, using evidence from regular observations, student data, and other sources to evaluate the effectiveness of teachers and staff.

  (ii) In schools with effective leaders of human capital, staff understand how they are being evaluated and what the expectations are for their performance. Staff can identify areas of strength and have opportunities to practice and receive feedback on growth areas from the leadership team and peers. Staff evaluation data show variation based on effectiveness but also show improvement across years as development and retention efforts take effect. Across the school, staff support each other's development through regular opportunities for collaboration, and effective staff have access to a variety of leadership roles in the school.

(B) Indicators.

  (i) Targeted selection, placement, and retention. The principal selects, places, and retains effective staff.

  (ii) Tailored development, feedback, and coaching. The principal coaches and develops teachers by giving individualized feedback and aligned professional development opportunities.

(iii) Staff collaboration and leadership. The principal implements collaborative structures and provides leadership opportunities for effective teachers and staff.

(iv) Systematic evaluation and supervision. The principal conducts rigorous evaluations of all staff multiple data sources.

(3) Standard 3—Executive Leadership. The principal is responsible for modeling a consistent focus on and commitment to improving student learning.

(A) Knowledge and skills.

(i) Effective executive leaders:

(I) are committed to ensuring the success of the school;

(II) motivate the school community by modeling a relentless pursuit of excellence;

(III) are reflective in their practice and strive to continually improve, learn, and grow;

(IV) view unsuccessful experiences as learning opportunities, focused on solutions, and are not stymied by challenges or setbacks. When a strategy fails, these principals analyze data, assess implementation, and talk with stakeholders to understand what went wrong and how to adapt strategies moving forward;

(V) keep staff inspired and focused on the end goal even as they support effective change management;

(VI) have strong communication skills and understand how to communicate a message in different ways to meet the needs of various audiences;

(VII) are willing to listen to others and create opportunities for staff and stakeholders to provide feedback; and

(VIII) treat all members of the community with respect and develop strong, positive relationships with them.

(ii) In schools with effective executive leaders, teachers and staff are motivated and committed to excellence. They are vested in the school's improvement and participate in candid discussions of progress and challenges. They are comfortable providing feedback to the principal and other school leaders in pursuit of ongoing improvement, and they welcome feedback from students' families in support of improved student outcomes.

(B) Indicators.

(i) Resiliency and change management. The principal remains solutions-oriented, treats challenges as opportunities, and supports staff through changes.

(ii) Commitment to ongoing learning. The principal proactively seeks and acts on feedback, reflects on personal growth areas and seeks development opportunities, and accepts responsibility for mistakes.

(iii) Communication and interpersonal skills. The principal tailors communication strategies to the audience and develops meaningful and positive relationships.

(iv) Ethical behavior. The principal adheres to the educators' code of ethics in §247.2 of this title relating to Code of Ethics and Standard Practices for Texas Educators, including following policies and procedures at his or her respective district.

(4) Standard 4—School Culture. The principal is responsible for establishing and implementing a shared vision and culture of high expectations for all staff and students.

(A) Knowledge and skills.

(i) Effective culture leaders:

(I) leverage school culture to drive improved outcomes and create high expectations;

(II) establish and implement a shared vision of high achievement for all students and use that vision as the foundation for key decisions and priorities for the school;

(III) establish and communicate consistent expectations for staff and students, providing supportive feedback to ensure a positive campus environment;

(IV) focus on students' social and emotional development and help students develop resiliency and self-advocacy skills; and

(V) treat families as key partners to support student learning, creating structures for two-way communication and regular updates on student progress. Regular opportunities exist for both families and the community to engage with the school and participate in school functions.

(ii) In schools with effective culture leaders, staff believe in and are inspired by the school vision and have high expectations for all students. Staff take responsibility for communicating the vision in their classrooms and for implementing behavioral expectations throughout the building, not only in their own classrooms. Teachers regularly communicate with the families of their students to provide updates on progress and actively work with families to support learning at home. Members of the broader community regularly engage with the school community.

(B) Indicators.

    (i) Shared vision of high achievement. The principal develops and implements a shared vision of high expectations for students and staff.

    (ii) Culture of high expectations. The principal establishes and monitors clear expectations for adult and student conduct and implements social and emotional supports for students.

    (iii) Intentional family and community engagement. The principal engages families and community members in student learning.

    (iv) Safe school environment. The principal creates an atmosphere of safety that encourages the social, emotional, and physical well-being of staff and students.

    (v) Discipline. The principal oversees an orderly environment, maintaining expectations for student behavior while implementing a variety of student discipline techniques to meet the needs of individual students.

(5) Standard 5—Strategic Operations. The principal is responsible for implementing systems that align with the school's vision and improve the quality of instruction.

(A) Knowledge and skills.

    (i) Effective leaders of strategic operations:

        (I) assess the current needs of their schools, reviewing a wide set of evidence to determine the schools' priorities and set ambitious and measurable school goals, targets, and strategies that form the schools' strategic plans;

        (II) with their leadership teams, regularly monitor multiple data points to evaluate progress toward goals, adjusting strategies that are proving ineffective;

(III) develop a year-long calendar and a daily schedule that strategically use time to both maximize instructional time and to create regular time for teacher collaboration and data review;

(IV) are deliberate in the allocation of resources (e.g., staff time, dollars, and tools), aligning them to the school priorities and goals, and work to access additional resources as needed to support learning; and

(V) treat central office staff as partners in achieving goals and collaborate with staff throughout district to adapt policies as needed to meet the needs of students and staff.

(ii) In schools with effective leaders of strategic operations, staff have access to resources needed to meet the needs of all students. Staff understand the goals and expectations for students, have clear strategies for meeting those goals, and have the capacity to track progress. Members of the staff collaborate with the principal to develop the school calendar. Teacher teams and administrator teams meet regularly to review and improve instructional strategies and analyze student data. Throughout the year, all staff participate in formal development opportunities that build the capacity to identify and implement strategies aligned to the school's improvement goals.

(B) Indicators.

(i) Strategic planning. The principal outlines and tracks clear goals, targets, and strategies aligned to a school vision that improves teacher effectiveness and student outcomes.

(ii) Maximized learning time. The principal implements daily schedules and a year-long calendar that plan for regular data-driven instruction cycles, give students access to diverse and rigorous course offerings, and build in time for staff professional development.

(iii) Tactical resource management. The principal aligns resources with the needs of the school and effectively monitors the impact on school goals.

(iv) Policy implementation and advocacy. The principal collaborates with district staff to implement and advocate for district policies that meet the needs of students and staff.

Statutory Authority: The provisions of this §149.2001 issued under the Texas Education Code, §21.3541.

Source: The provisions of this §149.2001 adopted to be effective June 8, 2014, 39 TexReg 4245, ritter.tea.state.tx.us/rules/tac/chapter149/ch14966. html.

Appendix 3

Texas Standards/Competencies for the Principal—Test Framework

Domain I—School Community Leadership
Domain II—Instructional Leadership
Domain III—Administrative Leadership

DOMAIN I—SCHOOL COMMUNITY LEADERSHIP

Competency 001

The principal knows how to shape campus culture by facilitating the development, articulation, implementation, and stewardship of a vision of learning that is shared and supported by the school community.
The principal knows how to:

1. create a campus culture that sets high expectations, promotes learning, and provides intellectual stimulation for self, students, and staff.
2. ensure that parents and other members of the community are an integral part of the campus culture.
3. implement strategies to ensure the development of collegial relationships and effective collaboration.
4. respond appropriately to diverse needs in shaping the campus culture.
5. use various types of information (e.g., demographic data, campus climate inventory results, student achievement data, emerging issues af-

fecting education) to develop a campus vision and create a plan for implementing the vision.

6. use strategies for involving all stakeholders in planning processes to enable the collaborative development of a shared campus vision focused on teaching and learning.
7. facilitate the collaborative development of a plan that clearly articulates objectives and strategies for implementing a campus vision.
8. align financial, human, and material resources to support implementation of a campus vision.
9. establish procedures to assess and modify implementation plans to ensure achievement of the campus vision.
10. support innovative thinking and risk taking within the school community and view unsuccessful experiences as learning opportunities.
11. acknowledge and celebrate the contributions of students, staff, parents, and community members toward realization of the campus vision.

Competency 002

The principal knows how to communicate and collaborate with all members of the school community, respond to diverse interests and needs, and mobilize resources to promote student success.

The principal knows how to:

1. communicate effectively with families and other community members in varied educational contexts.
2. apply skills for building consensus and managing conflict.
3. implement effective strategies for systematically communicating with and gathering input from all campus stakeholders.
4. develop and implement strategies for effective internal and external communications.
5. develop and implement a comprehensive program of community relations that effectively involves and informs multiple constituencies, including the media.
6. provide varied and meaningful opportunities for parents/caregivers to be engaged in the education of their children.
7. establish partnerships with parents/caregivers, businesses, and others in the community to strengthen programs and support campus goals.

8. communicate and work effectively with diverse groups in the school community to ensure that all students have an equal opportunity for educational success.
9. respond to pertinent political, social, and economic issues in the internal and external environment.

Competency 003

The principal knows how to act with integrity, fairness, and in an ethical and legal manner.

The principal knows how to:

1. model and promote the highest standard of conduct, ethical principles, and integrity in decision making, actions, and behaviors.
2. implement policies and procedures that promote professional educator compliance with the Code of Ethics and Standard Practices for Texas Educators.
3. apply knowledge of ethical issues affecting education.
4. apply legal guidelines (e.g., in relation to students with disabilities, bilingual education, confidentiality, discrimination) to protect the rights of students and staff and to improve learning opportunities.
5. apply laws, policies, and procedures in a fair and reasonable manner.
6. articulate the importance of education in a free democratic society.
7. serve as an advocate for all children.
8. promote the continuous and appropriate development of all students.
9. promote awareness of learning differences, multicultural awareness, gender sensitivity, and ethnic appreciation.

DOMAIN II INSTRUCTIONAL LEADERSHIP

Competency 004

The principal knows how to facilitate the design and implementation of curricula and strategic plans that enhance teaching and learning; ensure alignment of curriculum, instruction, resources, and assessment; and promote the use of varied assessments to measure student performance.

The principal knows how to:

1. facilitate effective campus curriculum planning based on knowledge of various factors (e.g., emerging issues, occupational and economic trends, demographic data, student learning data, motivation theory, teaching and learning theory, principles of curriculum design, human developmental processes, legal requirements).
2. facilitate the use of sound, research-based practice in the development, implementation, and evaluation of campus curricular, co-curricular, and extracurricular programs.
3. facilitate campus participation in collaborative district planning, implementation, monitoring, and revision of curriculum to ensure appropriate scope, sequence, content, and alignment.
4. facilitate the use of appropriate assessments to measure student learning and ensure educational accountability.
5. facilitate the use of technology, telecommunications, and information systems to enrich the campus curriculum.
6. facilitate the effective coordination of campus curricular, co-curricular, and extracurricular programs in relation to other district programs.
7. promote the use of creative thinking, critical thinking, and problem solving by staff and other campus stakeholders involved in curriculum design and delivery.

Competency 005

The principal knows how to advocate, nurture, and sustain an instructional program and a campus culture that are conducive to student learning and staff professional growth.

The principal knows how to:

1. facilitate the development of a campus learning organization that supports instructional improvement and change through ongoing study of relevant research and best practice.
2. facilitate the implementation of sound, research-based instructional strategies, decisions, and programs in which multiple opportunities to learn and be successful are available to all students.
3. create conditions that encourage staff, students, families/caregivers, and the community to strive to achieve the campus vision.
4. ensure that all students are provided high-quality, flexible instructional programs with appropriate resources and services to meet individual student needs.

5. use formative and summative student assessment data to develop, support, and improve campus instructional strategies and goals.
6. facilitate the use and integration of technology, telecommunications, and information systems to enhance learning.
7. facilitate the implementation of sound, research-based theories and techniques of teaching, learning, classroom management, student discipline, and school safety to ensure a campus environment conducive to teaching and learning.
8. facilitate the development, implementation, evaluation, and refinement of student services and activity programs to fulfill academic, developmental, social, and cultural needs.
9. analyze instructional needs and allocate resources effectively and equitably.
10. analyze the implications of various factors (e.g., staffing patterns, class scheduling formats, school organizational structures, student discipline practices) for teaching and learning.
11. ensure responsiveness to diverse sociological, linguistic, cultural, and other factors that may affect students' development and learning.

Competency 006

The principal knows how to implement appropriate models for supervision and staff development, and apply the legal requirements for personnel management.
The principal knows how to:

1. work collaboratively with other campus personnel to develop, implement, evaluate, and revise a comprehensive campus professional development plan that addresses staff needs and aligns professional development with identified goals.
2. facilitate the application of adult learning principles and motivation theory to all campus professional development activities, including the use of appropriate content, processes, and contexts.
3. allocate appropriate time, funding, and other needed resources to ensure the effective implementation of professional development plans.
4. implement effective, appropriate, and legal strategies for the recruitment, screening, selection, assignment, induction, development, evaluation, promotion, discipline, and dismissal of campus staff.

5. use formative and summative evaluation procedures to enhance the knowledge and skills of campus staff.
6. diagnose campus organizational health and morale and implement strategies to provide ongoing support to campus staff.
7. engage in ongoing professional development activities to enhance one's own knowledge and skills and to model lifelong learning.

Competency 007

The principal knows how to apply organizational decision-making and problem-solving skills to ensure an effective learning environment.
The principal knows how to:

1. implement appropriate management techniques and group process skills to define roles, assign functions, delegate authority, and determine accountability for campus goal attainment.
2. implement procedures for gathering, analyzing, and using data from a variety of sources for informed campus decision making.
3. frame, analyze, and resolve problems using appropriate problem-solving techniques and decision-making skills.
4. use strategies for promoting collaborative decision making and problem solving, facilitating team building, and developing consensus.
5. encourage and facilitate positive change, enlist support for change, and overcome obstacles to change.
6. apply skills for monitoring and evaluating change and making needed adjustments to achieve goals.

DOMAIN III—ADMINISTRATIVE LEADERSHIP

Competency 008

The principal knows how to apply principles of effective leadership and management in relation to campus budgeting, personnel, resource utilization, financial management, and technology use.
The principal knows how to:

1. apply procedures for effective budget planning and management.
2. work collaboratively with stakeholders to develop campus budgets.

3. acquire, allocate, and manage human, material, and financial resources according to district policies and campus priorities.
4. apply laws and policies to ensure sound financial management in relation to accounts, bidding, purchasing, and grants.
5. use effective planning, time management, and organization of personnel to maximize attainment of district and campus goals.
6. develop and implement plans for using technology and information systems to enhance school management.

Competency 009

The principal knows how to apply principles of leadership and management to the campus physical plant and support systems to ensure a safe and effective learning environment.

The principal knows how to:

1. implement strategies that enable the school physical plant, equipment, and support systems to operate safely, efficiently, and effectively.
2. apply strategies for ensuring the safety of students and personnel and for addressing emergencies and security concerns.
3. develop and implement procedures for crisis planning and for responding to crises.
4. apply local, state, and federal laws and policies to support sound decision making related to school programs and operations (e.g., student services, food services, transportation).

NOTE

School community: Includes students, staff, parents/caregivers, and community members.

Source: TEA. 2010. State Board for Educator Certification, TExES Texas Examination of Educator Standards, Prep Manual. Available at cms.texes-ets.org/files/1413/2949/6303/068_principal.pdf.

Appendix 4

Texas Administrative Code, Title 19, Part 7, Chapter 247, Rule §247.2

ENFORCEABLE STANDARDS

(1) Professional Ethical Conduct, Practices and Performance.

   (A) Standard 1.1. The educator shall not intentionally, knowingly, or recklessly engage in deceptive practices regarding official policies of the school district, educational institution, educator preparation program, the Texas Education Agency, or the State Board for Educator Certification (SBEC) and its certification process.

   (B) Standard 1.2. The educator shall not knowingly misappropriate, divert, or use monies, personnel, property, or equipment committed to his or her charge for personal gain or advantage.

   (C) Standard 1.3. The educator shall not submit fraudulent requests for reimbursement, expenses, or pay.

   (D) Standard 1.4. The educator shall not use institutional or professional privileges for personal or partisan advantage.

   (E) Standard 1.5. The educator shall neither accept nor offer gratuities, gifts, or favors that impair professional judgment or to obtain special advantage. This standard shall not restrict the acceptance of gifts or tokens offered and accepted openly from students, parents of students, or other persons or organizations in recognition or appreciation of service.

(F) Standard 1.6. The educator shall not falsify records, or direct or coerce others to do so.

(G) Standard 1.7. The educator shall comply with state regulations, written local school board policies, and other state and federal laws.

(H) Standard 1.8. The educator shall apply for, accept, offer, or assign a position or a responsibility on the basis of professional qualifications.

(I) Standard 1.9. The educator shall not make threats of violence against school district employees, school board members, students, or parents of students.

(J) Standard 1.10. The educator shall be of good moral character and be worthy to instruct or supervise the youth of this state.

(K) Standard 1.11. The educator shall not intentionally or knowingly misrepresent his or her employment history, criminal history, and/or disciplinary record when applying for subsequent employment.

(L) Standard 1.12. The educator shall refrain from the illegal use or distribution of controlled substances and/or abuse of prescription drugs and toxic inhalants.

(M) Standard 1.13. The educator shall not consume alcoholic beverages on school property or during school activities when students are present.

(2) Ethical Conduct toward Professional Colleagues.

(A) Standard 2.1. The educator shall not reveal confidential health or personnel information concerning colleagues unless disclosure serves lawful professional purposes or is required by law.

(B) Standard 2.2. The educator shall not harm others by knowingly making false statements about a colleague or the school system.

(C) Standard 2.3. The educator shall adhere to written local school board policies and state and federal laws regarding the hiring, evaluation, and dismissal of personnel.

(D)Standard 2.4. The educator shall not interfere with a colleague's exercise of political, professional, or citizenship rights and responsibilities.

(E) Standard 2.5. The educator shall not discriminate against or coerce a colleague on the basis of race, color, religion, national origin, age, gender, disability, family status, or sexual orientation.

(F) Standard 2.6. The educator shall not use coercive means or promise of special treatment in order to influence professional decisions or colleagues.

(G) Standard 2.7. The educator shall not retaliate against any individual who has filed a complaint with the SBEC or who provides information for a disciplinary investigation or proceeding under this chapter.

(3) Ethical Conduct toward Students.

(A) Standard 3.1. The educator shall not reveal confidential information concerning students unless disclosure serves lawful professional purposes or is required by law.

(B) Standard 3.2. The educator shall not intentionally, knowingly, or recklessly treat a student or minor in a manner that adversely affects or endangers the learning, physical health, mental health, or safety of the student or minor.

(C) Standard 3.3. The educator shall not intentionally, knowingly, or recklessly misrepresent facts regarding a student.

(D) Standard 3.4. The educator shall not exclude a student from participation in a program, deny benefits to a student, or grant an advantage to a student on the basis of race, color, gender, disability, national origin, religion, family status, or sexual orientation.

(E) Standard 3.5. The educator shall not intentionally, knowingly, or recklessly engage in physical mistreatment, neglect, or abuse of a student or minor.

(F) Standard 3.6. The educator shall not solicit or engage in sexual conduct or a romantic relationship with a student or minor.

(G) Standard 3.7. The educator shall not furnish alcohol or illegal/unauthorized drugs to any person under twenty-one years of age unless the educator is a parent or guardian of that child or knowingly allow any person under twenty-one years of age unless the educator is a parent or guardian of that child to consume alcohol or illegal/unauthorized drugs in the presence of the educator.

(H) Standard 3.8. The educator shall maintain appropriate professional educator-student relationships and boundaries based on a reasonably prudent educator standard.

(I) Standard 3.9. The educator shall refrain from inappropriate communication with a student or minor, including, but not limited to, electronic communication such as cell phone, text messaging, email, instant messaging, blogging, or other social network communication. Factors that may be considered in assessing whether the communication is inappropriate include, but are not limited to:

(i) the nature, purpose, timing, and amount of the communication;

(ii) the subject matter of the communication;

(iii) whether the communication was made openly or the educator attempted to conceal the communication;

(iv) whether the communication could be reasonably interpreted as soliciting sexual contact or a romantic relationship;

(v) whether the communication was sexually explicit; and

(vi) whether the communication involved discussion(s) of the physical or sexual attractiveness or the sexual history, activities, preferences, or fantasies of either the educator or the student.

NOTE

Source Note: The provisions of this §247.2 adopted to be effective March 1, 1998, 23 TexReg 1022; amended to be effective August 22, 2002, 27 TexReg 7530; amended to be effective December 26, 2010, 35 TexReg 11242. Available at: tea.texas.gov/index2.aspx?id= 2147501244&menu_id=771&menu_id2=794.

About the Authors

Sandra Harris has been an educator for over forty years in public and private schools in Maryland, Kansas, and Texas. During that time, she has been a teacher, principal, superintendent, and university professor. Currently, she is professor and dissertation coordinator at Lamar University in Beaumont, Texas. Harris earned her PhD from the University of Texas at Austin in educational leadership. She has served in leadership roles in several organizations, such as former executive board member and president of the National Council of Professors of Educational Administration (NCPEA), and former president of the Texas Council of Professors of Educational Administrations (TCPEA). Dr. Harris has been the recipient of the NCPEA Living Legend award and also the TCPEA Vornberg Living Legend award. She has authored or coauthored twenty-two books, and presented and published widely in educational journals, and contributed many chapters in books regarding school leadership.

Julia Ballenger received her PhD in educational administration from the University of Texas at Austin. She has worked as a public school teacher, administrator, counselor, consultant, state agency director, and higher education professor for over forty years. Dr. Ballenger is currently employed at Texas A&M University in Commerce, where she teaches in the educational leadership doctoral and master's programs. She has served in leadership roles in several organizations, such as former executive board member of the National Council of Professors of Educational Administration (NCPEA), former president of the Texas Council of Professors of Educational Administrations, executive board member of the Southwest Educational Research Association, member of the University Council of Educational Administration Taskforce for Principal Preparation, former president and board member of the Research on Women and Education SIG, AERA, and member of the American Educational Research Association. Ballenger's research agenda includes: Principal Preparation Program Evaluation, Mentoring and Higher Educational Leadership, Evaluation of Online Higher Education Doctoral and Masters' Programs, Leadership for Social Justice, and Cultural Responsive Pedagogy.

Cynthia Cummings received her EdD in educational administration from Lamar University. Dr. Cummings has served as a classroom teacher, administrator, consultant, and professor over the past twenty years. In addition to her work with classroom teachers, she has extensive experience providing professional development for school leaders. She worked with Texas principals and superintendents in a technology leadership project funded by the Bill and Melinda Gates Foundation. She was instrumental in establishing the Brazos-Sabine Connection Principal Academy, whose goal was to provide school leaders with the skills needed to support effective integration of teaching, learning, and technology. Currently, she is employed as an assistant professor and director of principal programs at Lamar University in Beaumont, Texas. Her responsibilities include writing and teaching online graduate-level courses and directing the master's level principal program. Dr. Cummings' research interests include professional development, distance education, technology integration, global leadership, and electronic portfolios.